Good Housekeeping

# FAMILY
# vegetarian
# COOKING

**225** Recipes
Everyone Will Love

# FAMILY
# vegetarian
# COOKING

**225** Recipes
**Everyone Will Love**

HEARST BOOKS
A division of Sterling Publishing Co., Inc.

New York / London
**www.sterlingpublishing.com**

GOOD HOUSEKEEPING

| | |
|---|---|
| Rosemary Ellis | *Editor in Chief* |
| Sara Lyle | *Lifestyle Editor* |
| Susan Westmoreland | *Food Director* |
| Samantha Cassetty | *Nutrition Director* |
| Sharon Franke | *Food Appliances Director* |

*Editor:* Pam Hoenig
*Production Editor:* Sarah Scheffel
*Book Designer:* Anna Christian
Photography Credits on page 279

Library of Congress Cataloging-in-Publication Data

Family vegetarian cooking : 225 recipes everyone will love.
    p. cm.
  At head of title Good housekeeping
  Includes index.
  ISBN-13: 978-1-58816-792-7
  ISBN-10: 1-58816-792-5
1. Vegetarian cookery. 2. Vegetarianism—Popular works. 3. Nutrition—Popular works. I. Good housekeeping (New York, N.Y.) II. Title: Good housekeeping family vegetarian cooking. III. Title: Good housekeeping.
  TX837.F254 2009
  641.5'636—dc22
                              2010037911

10 9 8 7 6 5 4 3 2 1

The Good Housekeeping Cookbook Seal guarantees that the recipes in this cookbook meet the strict standards of the Good Housekeeping Research Institute. The Institute has been a source of reliable information and a consumer advocate since 1900, and established its seal of approval in 1909. Every recipe has been triple-tested for ease, reliability, and great taste.

Published by Hearst Books
A division of Sterling Publishing Co., Inc.
387 Park Avenue South, New York, NY 10016

Good Housekeeping is a registered trademark of Hearst Communications, Inc.

www.goodhousekeeping.com

For information about custom editions, special sales, premium and corporate purchases, please contact Sterling Special Sales Department at 800-805-5489 or specialsales@sterlingpublishing.com.

Distributed in Canada by Sterling Publishing
c/o Canadian Manda Group, 165 Dufferin Street
Toronto, Ontario, Canada M6K 3H6

Distributed in Australia by Capricorn Link (Australia) Pty. Ltd.
P.O. Box 704, Windsor, NSW 2756 Australia

Manufactured in China

Sterling ISBN 978-1-58816-792-7

*Spaghetti with Pesto and Tomato-Mozzarella Salad (page 208)*

# Contents

Foreword **8**
Introduction **10**

1 Breakfast & Brunch **16**

2 Pizzas, Sandwiches & Burgers **40**

3 Salad Makes the Meal **60**

4 Soups, Stews & Chilis **86**

5 Stir-Fries & Sautés **126**

6 Hot from the Oven **144**

7 Veggies on the Grill **180**

8 Pasta, Rice & Grains **202**

9 The Flexible Vegetarian **228**

10 Sweet & Fruity Desserts **246**

Metric Equivalent Charts **278**
Photography Credits **279**
Index **279**

# Foreword

Like most mothers, I am always on the lookout for delicious healthful meals to feed my family. Unlike most mothers, I have the opportunity of tasting new recipes for these meals every day in the Good Housekeeping Test Kitchens. What I'm looking for more and more are dinners where whole grains, legumes, vegetables, and fruits take center stage. Studies show that eating meals rich in these ingredients (and low in fat) can lower the risk of illnesses like diabetes and heart disease. This is not information my husband or teenage son are particularly interested in—unless the food happens to be delicious.

Once I get the silent treatment (in our house this means everyone's focused on eating) or the *mmmm* good, I do full disclosure of ingredients. I pride myself on choosing the freshest ingredients (my grandfather owned a produce market, and he taught me everything I know about picking vegetables and fruits), so the boys humor me as I gleefully report: golden cauliflower from the farmers' market, first local asparagus, apples from Tara's tree. Our goal at *Good Housekeeping* as we developed this cookbook was to keep flavor profiles rich—and familiar—and deliver real family-friendly food, so you'll have plenty of options for delicious vegetarian meals that your family will relate to and enjoy!

Whether your family eats vegetarian exclusively or just a few meals a week, *Family Vegetarian Cooking* serves up lots of satisfying options—225 of them to be exact. You'll find flavorful vegetarian takes on foods everyone loves, from hearty chilis and tempting stir-fries to classic casseroles and easy-to-make pizzas, burritos, and more. Hearty breakfast and brunch fare such as 5-Minute Multigrain Cereal and South-of-the-Border Vegetable Hash are a great start to any day. And our easy and yummy wraps, sandwiches, and veggie burgers make perfect lunches. Any of our salads, or a bowl of one of our warming soups, stews, or chilis (I stash leftovers in single-serving containers and freeze for use on Mom's night out or for teenager-worthy snacks) are also great ways to serve up healthful ingredients at lunchtime.

And then it's on to dinner, including a cornucopia of stir-fries and sautés (such as curries and lo meins to replace expensive takeout) that can be done in under 30 minutes; casseroles and other hot-from-the-oven dishes (from lasagnas to gratins to Macaroni and Cheese Deluxe); pasta, rice, and grain dishes galore; and even vegetarian specialties for the grill. Southwestern Black-Bean Burgers hot from the grill are a hearty lunch, or made smaller, they make yummy appetizers. (My son decided he liked mushrooms after eating a Tomato, Portobello, and Mozzarella Melt.)

The Flexible Vegetarian chapter provides lots of options for nights when just one or two of your family members want a vegetarian dinner. These recipes allow you to serve essentially the same wholesome stir-fry, curry, salad, or pizza to your entire family, finishing with tofu or extra veggies for those who are eating vegetarian and a small amount of meat, poultry, or fish for the rest of the gang. Sprinkled throughout, you'll find tip boxes, called It's So Good!, on just how nutritious fruits and vegetables are. If you'd like to cut back on dairy in your diet, look for our special icon **V**, which identifies the many vegan recipes in this book, as well as the Make It Vegan tips sprinkled throughout.

Of course, some days we just need dessert—from frozen Chocolate-Dipped Banana Pops and Summer Fruit in Spiced Syrup to baked goodies like chunky oatmeal cookies and Apricot Upside-Down Cake, we've got dessert covered.

Whether you're cooking for seasoned vegetarians or scouting new ideas for weekly meatless dinners, *Family Vegetarian Cooking* will make it easy to prepare good-for-you meals that everyone will love. So pick up some fresh vegetables and fruits, peel and chop a few minutes, and cook up any of our triple-tested recipes. Then relax and enjoy dinner with your family.

—Susan Westmoreland
Food Director, *Good Housekeeping*

# Introduction

For generations, the mealtime mantra of mothers across America has been "Eat your vegetables!" As usual, Mom was right. In study after study, it has been shown that eating a diet rich in fruits, vegetables, whole grains, and legumes and low in fat results in numerous health benefits:

✦ It reduces the risk of some cancers.

✦ It lowers the incidence of diabetes.

✦ It reduces the possibility of stroke.

✦ It can lower LDL (or "bad") blood cholesterol.

✦ It reduces the risk of heart disease and can have a positive effect on the health of those who already have heart disease.

American's have finally gotten the message. Tens of millions of people in the U.S. have changed their eating habits to include more produce and grains and fewer animal products. In fact, according to a recent survey, while just 3% of Americans consider themselves vegetarians, more than 22% think of themselves as "vegetarian inclined."

## *Good Housekeeping* Introduces *Family Vegetarian Cooking*

We know there is any number of reasons you might have brought this book home:

✦ You're a vegetarian and you want a collection of family-friendly recipes that are easy to make and sure to satisfy and sustain your loved ones.

✦ You and your family are considering switching over to a vegetarian diet.

✦ Your son or daughter has just informed you that they're vegetarian, and you have few or no meatless recipes in your current mealtime repertoire.

## VEGGIES VS. SUPPLEMENTS

Researchers have long known that people who eat a plant-based diet have a strikingly lower risk for heart disease, cancer, and other chronic diseases—and that vitamin and mineral supplements don't seem to offer the same potent protection. Why is that?

Plant foods and whole grains contain hundreds, if not thousands, of phytochemicals, substances that are neither vitamins nor minerals. Scientists have found some of these compounds lend fruits and vegetables their vibrant colors; others are part of the plant's defense system against bacteria and insects. Now, ever-growing research suggests that these chemicals protect us, too—from many of the disorders of aging. And although we're still learning about all of the mechanisms by which these potent plant chemicals defend us, one thing is for sure: The only way to get them is by ingesting them in the form Mother Nature intended us to.

✦ None of your family members are vegetarian or intend to become vegetarians, but you want to start serving meatless meals once or twice a week because of the health benefits.

Whatever your motivation, *Family Vegetarian Cooking* is here to help. With more than 225 recipes developed in the *Good Housekeeping* kitchens with Mom in mind, this is a book you can rely on to feed your family with ease and confidence.

## Introducing the Vegetarian Diet

If you're considering becoming a vegetarian or have someone in your family who has just made this choice, you probably have questions, many of them nutritional, about what it means to be a vegetarian.

### Children and a Vegetarian Diet

If your ten year old has just come home and informed you that she will never eat meat again, there is no need for worry: The American Dietetic Association has stated that a properly planned vegetarian diet (including a vegan one) can provide all the nutrients necessary to sustain normal, healthy growth for children at all stages, from infant to adolescent. The key is being aware of the essential nutrients we derive from animal products and how they can be replaced by plant-based foods.

## Nutritional Guidelines for Vegetarians (and Vegans)

If you or someone in your family (especially growing children) is eliminating animal-based products from their diet, there are several nutrients you need to pay particular attention to:

PROTEIN: Protein is involved in most every type of cell function in the human body, including the production of antibodies and hemoglobin. When a child tells Mom that she's going to be a vegetarian, it's usually protein Mom is most worried about. But there is no need; there are plenty of plant-based sources for protein.

Here are a few: pumpkin seeds, peanuts, oats, lima beans, soybeans and soy-based products like tofu and soy milk (check the package's nutrition label; the amount of protein varies from brand to brand), and other legumes and pulses, including split peas, lentils, garbanzo beans, black beans, and pinto beans. If you're keeping dairy and eggs in your diet, yogurt, eggs, low-fat milk, and cheese are also good sources of protein.

CALCIUM: The mineral calcium is key to bone manufacture; it also aids in blood clotting and healthy nerve and muscle function. If you are following an entirely vegetarian or vegan diet, according to the North American Vegetarian Food Pyramid, you should be including 8 servings of calcium-containing food each day. Some

## SO WHAT ARE "COMPLETE" PROTEINS?

Protein is made up of 20 amino acids, 11 of which our body can manufacture on its own. The other nine have to be derived from food; because we can't make them ourselves, they are referred to as "essential" amino acids. You may hear of a food being referred to as a "complete" protein. That means it contains all nine of these essential amino acids in nutritionally significant quantities: animal proteins, such as meat, fish, and eggs, are considered complete proteins. Most all plant-based sources of protein are not considered complete, with the exception of soybeans and the grain quinoa.

The concept developed a number of decades ago that if you were following a vegetarian diet, you would need to eat foods in combination at the same meal that supplied all the essential amino acids required for good health. An example of such food combining would be lentils and rice, which each supply an amino acid that the other is low in.

Today it is understood that this kind of food combining isn't necessary. The key to getting the essential amino acids you need for good health is to eat a broad range of protein-rich food throughout the day (see the list in the section on protein). That way, if one food is low in a particular amino acid, it will be made up for by another food high in that acid.

of the best sources of calcium for those following a vegetarian diet are: yogurt, low-fat cheese and milk, soybeans and soy-based products like tofu and calcium-enriched soymilk, calcium-enriched orange juice, and sesame seeds. Spinach, collards greens, and Swiss chard also contain goodly amounts of calcium, but it is significantly less readily absorbed by the body, and thus should not be relied on as a primary source for calcium.

IRON: The mineral iron is essential because it enables red blood cells to carry oxygen throughout the body. There are two types of iron in food. One is found in meat and fish and is readily absorbed. The other type of iron is plant based, which is less well absorbed. However, when plant-based iron-rich foods are consumed in tandem with foods containing vitamin C (or if a particular food contains both iron and vitamin C, like Swiss chard), the absorption rate of the iron increases significantly. There are many vegetables that contain both (see the list below), but you can also create your own combinations, for example by simmering iron-rich tofu in a vitamin C-rich tomato sauce, or by adding vitamin C-packed bell peppers to a three-bean salad (legumes of all sorts are a great source of iron).

ZINC: While the body does not need much zinc, what it does need is vital for good health. The body's immune cells are dependent upon zinc for their optimal function, and zinc also plays an important part in the regulation of blood-sugar levels in the body and in maintaining our metabolic rate. Sources of zinc include pumpkin and sesame seeds, green peas, black beans, soybeans, lentils, garbanzo beans, yogurt, and cremini mushrooms.

VITAMIN $B_{12}$: Vitamin $B_{12}$ is vital to red blood cell production, as well as the development of nerve cells. It is predominantly derived from meat and fish products. In a vegetarian diet, it can be found in eggs and dairy products. In a vegan diet, it can be found in nutritional yeast, as well as $B_{12}$-fortified products such as cereal and soymilk (check your labels).

## The Vegetarian Food Groups

For a vegetarian or vegan, the key to good health is a varied diet of plant-based food representing a broad nutritional range. One model, the North American Vegetarian Food Pyramid developed by the American Dietetic Association, recommends eating these quantities daily from the following food groups. (Note: Serving sizes are specific to this model.)

✦ 6 servings of whole grains per day (a serving could be 1 slice of whole-grain bread, ½ cup of a cooked grain or cereal, or 1 ounce of ready-to-eat cereal)

✦ 5 servings of protein-rich foods per day (like ½ cup cooked legumes, ½ cup soy milk or cubed or crumbled tofu or tempeh, 2 tablespoons of a nut or seed butter (like peanut butter or tahini), ¼ cup nuts, 1 egg, ½ cup milk or yogurt, or ¾ ounce cheese

✦ 4 servings of vegetables per day (a serving would be ½ cup of a cooked vegetable, 1 cup of a raw veggie, or ½ cup of vegetable juice)

✦ 2 servings of fruit per day (a serving is 1 medium-size piece of fruit, ¼ cup dried fruit, or ½ cup pure fruit juice)

✦ 2 servings of fat per day. You may think you want to eliminate fat entirely from your diet, but the intake of some fat is essential to good health, particularly the health of growing children. A single serving would be 1 teaspoon of oil, mayonnaise, butter, or margarine.

And, according to the Pyramid, in making these selections, you want to make sure you're getting 8 servings of calcium-rich food per day. So, for instance, an eight-ounce glass of calcium-fortified orange juice would satisfy your fruit requirement while also filling at least two servings of your calcium requirement.

## What Is a Vegan?

When someone calls him- or herself a vegetarian, they generally mean that they don't eat meat, poultry, or fish and shellfish, but do eat dairy products and eggs. Such a person would more precisely be called an ovo-lacto vegetarian. A vegan is someone who eliminates all animal food products from their diet—no meat or dairy products, poultry or eggs, or fish and shellfish. There are a number of reasons people decide to become vegan, including:

✦ General health benefits

✦ Commitment to the humane treatment of animals

✦ Environmental concerns

✦ Food allergies or lactose intolerance

As with a vegetarian diet, there are many Americans who aren't vegans but who are considering making the change, or who would simply like to include egg- and dairy-free recipes in their

regular recipe rotation. For that reason, we've identified all the vegan recipes in this book with a special icon **V**. We've also included a special sidebar called Make It Vegan in cases where one small change in the ingredients turns a vegetarian recipe into a vegan one. An example would be a black bean soup that has a tablespoon of sour cream stirred in at the end. All you have to do is leave out the sour cream or use nondairy sour cream. Another instance would be a sandwich that includes mayonnaise; substitute soy mayonnaise and you have a vegan-friendly lunch.

## Eat and Enjoy!

Whatever your reason for wanting to cook meatless recipes, we invite you to explore the tasty selection of dishes we've assembled for you in *Family Vegetarian Cooking*. We've tried to pick recipes the whole family will enjoy while at the same time providing the good nutrition you want to serve up. And we've done our best to choose recipes that will fit into your busy schedule, whether you're looking for a casserole you can make ahead and freeze, or a quick stovetop dish to feed your family before rushing them off to their various activities.

Finally, we've included a chapter tailormade for a mom dealing with feeding a vegetarian child in an otherwise carnivorous family. Chapter 9, The Flexible Vegetarian, is filled with recipes that allow you to serve essentially the same meal to your whole family, reserving a vegetarian portion to feed one or several (sometimes rounded out by tofu or another soy protein) before adding meat, poultry, or fish or shellfish to the rest. Often a mom's first thought when a child says they're becoming a vegetarian is, am I going to have to make two dinners from now on? With the recipes in The Flexible Vegetarian, the answer is, of course not!

1

# Breakfast & Brunch

A good breakfast provides a solid foundation for healthy nutrition for the rest of the day—that is, if you select your menu wisely. If your breakfast of choice is ready-to-eat breakfast cereal, pick a cereal that contains lots of whole grains, a rich source of dietary fiber that helps to moderate blood sugar levels; sugar should *not* be one of the top three ingredients listed on the label.

But your breakfast needn't come from a box. In this chapter you'll find a selection of morning meals that are as delicious as they are nutritious. If you're interested in eating more whole grains, make sure you try our homemade granola and multigrain cereal recipes. When you think you have no time for breakfast, throw together one of our smoothies and take it to go. Those containing yogurt, milk, or soy milk will give you a healthy dose of protein and bone-building calcium.

We've also included a scrumptious array of egg dishes, from the classic omelet to an egg and bean burrito. Eggs are a high-quality source of protein (particularly the egg white) and incredibly versatile, so consider them your ally, especially if meat is not a regular part of your diet. Our crustless quiche and vegetable frittatas make for elegant vegetarian brunch fare, as do our French toast, pancakes, and sweet cherry-topped bruschetta.

*Clockwise from top left: Granola-Yogurt Parfait (page 22); Crustless Leek and Gruyère Quiche (page 33); Blueberry Pancakes with Warm Blueberry Sauce (page 36); Classic Cheese Omelet (page 24)*

# Orange Sunrise Smoothie Ⓥ

*Make this once and you'll want it to start all your mornings. If you don't have soy milk, you can substitute low-fat milk.*

**TOTAL TIME:** 5 minutes

**MAKES:** 1¾ cups or 1 serving

 1 cup vanilla soy milk
 ¼ cup frozen orange juice concentrate
 2 tablespoons orange marmalade
 2 ice cubes

In blender, combine soy milk, orange juice concentrate, marmalade, and ice, and blend until mixture is smooth and frothy. Pour into a tall glass.

**EACH SERVING:** About 360 calories, 8g protein, 73g carbohydrate, 5g fat (0g saturated), 2g fiber, 0mg cholesterol, 144mg sodium

# Mango-Strawberry Smoothie

*Whether you pair the strawberries with mango or apricot nectar, an irresistible flavor combination is the result. If you use frozen berries, skip the ice cubes.*

**TOTAL TIME:** 5 minutes

**MAKES:** 2½ cups or 2 servings

 1 cup fresh or frozen unsweetened strawberries
 1 cup mango or apricot nectar, chilled
 ½ cup plain or vanilla low-fat yogurt
 4 ice cubes

In blender, combine strawberries, nectar, yogurt, and ice, and blend until mixture is smooth and frothy. Pour into two tall glasses. Serve with straws, if you like.

**EACH SERVING:** About 130 calories, 4g protein, 27g carbohydrate, 1g total fat (1g saturated), 3g fiber, 3mg cholesterol, 44mg sodium

**DOUBLE-PEACH SMOOTHIE:** Substitute *peeled, pitted, and sliced peaches* for the strawberries and *peach juice or nectar* instead of mango or apricot nectar. Use *vanilla low-fat yogurt* and *3 ice cubes.*

**EACH SERVING:** About 160 calories, 3g protein, 36g carbohydrate, 1g total fat (1g saturated), 2g fiber, 3mg cholesterol, 45mg sodium

Ⓥ MAKE IT VEGAN: *Substitute nondairy yogurt.*

## Pomegranate-Berry Smoothie

*What a delicious and healthful way to start the day! Berries and pomegranates are loaded with heart-healthy antioxidants.*

**TOTAL TIME:** 5 minutes

**MAKES:** 2 cups or 1 serving

½ cup pomegranate juice, chilled
½ cup vanilla low-fat yogurt
1 cup frozen mixed berries

In blender, combine juice, yogurt, and berries, and blend until mixture is smooth. Pour into a tall glass.

**EACH SERVING:** About 250 calories, 6g protein, 52g carbohydrate, 2g total fat (1g saturated), 5g fiber, 8mg cholesterol, 110mg sodium

Ⓥ MAKE IT VEGAN: *Substitute nondairy yogurt.*

## Chocolate-Banana Smoothie

*Kids love the combo of chocolate and bananas. Plus, this breakfast drink is so easy to make, they can do it themselves.*

**TOTAL TIME:** 5 minutes

**MAKES:** 2 cups or 1 serving

1 peeled, sliced banana, frozen
¾ cup milk
3 tablespoons (or to taste) chocolate syrup
3 or 4 ice cubes

In blender, combine banana, milk, chocolate syrup, and ice, and blend until mixture is smooth and frothy. Pour into a tall glass.

**EACH SERVING:** About 430 calories, 9g protein, 85g carbohydrate, 8g total fat (4g saturated), 4g fiber, 25mg cholesterol, 145mg sodium

Ⓥ MAKE IT VEGAN: *Substitute soy milk. Be sure to select a chocolate syrup that does not contain milk solids.*

*5-Minute Multigrain Cereal*

# 5-Minute Multigrain Cereal ⓥ

*Get a great-grains start to your day with a hot and tasty serving of three kinds of grains in five minutes. Serve it with your choice of regular, soy, or rice milk.*

**ACTIVE TIME:** 5 minutes | **TOTAL TIME:** 10 minutes

**MAKES:** 1 serving

2 tablespoons quick-cooking barley
2 tablespoons bulgur (cracked wheat)
2 tablespoons old-fashioned oats
⅔ cup water
2 tablespoons raisins
pinch ground cinnamon
1 tablespoon chopped walnuts or pecans

In microwave-safe 1-quart bowl, combine barley, bulgur, oats, and water. Microwave on High 2 minutes. Stir in raisins and cinnamon; microwave 3 minutes longer. Stir, then top with walnuts.

**EACH SERVING:** About 265 calories, 8g protein, 50g carbohydrate, 6g total fat (1g saturated), 7g fiber, 0mg cholesterol, 5mg sodium

## COOK'S TIP

Recipes calling for a microwave were tested in a 1,100-watt microwave oven. If your microwave has more or less power, it may be necessary to make adjustments in cooking times to reach desired doneness.

# Cherry Bruschetta

*It's best to make this when sweet cherries are in season. Look for firm, plump fruit with stems attached, and a dark, almost blackberry-like color. This is a deliciously different choice for breakfast, and your guests won't complain one bit if you serve it up for dessert!*

**TOTAL TIME:** 10 minutes plus 15 minutes standing

**MAKES:** 4 servings

12 ounces fresh cherries, pitted and each cut in half
1 tablespoon sugar
1 teaspoon fresh lemon juice
4 slices (¾ inch thick) rustic bread
½ cup softened Neufchâtel or mascarpone cheese or thick Greek yogurt

1. In medium bowl, toss cherries, sugar, and lemon juice. Let stand 15 minutes to allow juices to run.

2. Lightly toast bread; cool slightly. Spread bread with cheese. Cut slices in half and arrange on platter; spoon cherries with juices on top.

**EACH SERVING:** About 255 calories, 7g protein, 38g carbohydrate, 9g total fat (5g saturated), 3g fiber, 21mg cholesterol, 370mg sodium

# Lower-Fat Granola ●V

*We baked oats, almonds, quinoa, wheat germ, and sesame seeds with apple juice instead of oil and butter. It's still got all that crunchy granola goodness but with just a fraction of the fat.*

**ACTIVE TIME:** 10 minutes | **TOTAL TIME:** 45 minutes
**MAKES:** 6 cups or 24 servings

4 cups old-fashioned oats
½ cup honey
½ cup apple juice
1½ teaspoons vanilla extract
¾ teaspoon ground cinnamon
½ cup natural almonds
½ cup quinoa
¼ cup toasted wheat germ
2 tablespoons sesame seeds
½ cup dried apricots, cut into ¼-inch dice
½ cup dark raisins

1. Preheat oven to 350°F. Place oats in two 15½" by 10½" jelly-roll pans. Bake oats until lightly toasted, about 15 minutes, stirring twice.

2. In large bowl, with wire whisk, mix honey, apple juice, vanilla, and cinnamon until blended. Add toasted oats, almonds, quinoa, wheat germ, and sesame seeds; stir well to coat.

3. Spread oat mixture evenly in same jelly-roll pans; bake until golden brown, 20 to 25 minutes, stirring frequently. Cool in pans on wire rack.

4. When cool, transfer to large bowl; stir in apricots and raisins. Store at room temperature in tightly covered container up to 1 month.

**EACH ¼ CUP SERVING:** About 175 calories, 6g protein, 32g carbohydrate, 4g total fat (1g saturated), 4g fiber, 0mg cholesterol, 5mg sodium

# Granola-Yogurt Parfait

*A healthy breakfast doesn't get any easier (or more delicious) than this.*

**TOTAL TIME:** 5 minutes
**MAKES:** 1 serving

½ cup fresh or frozen (partially thawed) raspberries or other favorite berry
¾ cup vanilla low-fat yogurt
2 tablespoons lower-fat granola

Into parfait glass or wineglass, spoon some of the raspberries, yogurt, and granola. Repeat layering until all ingredients are used.

**EACH SERVING:** About 255 calories, 10g protein, 47g carbohydrate, 3g total fat (2g saturated), 5g fiber, 12mg cholesterol, 160mg sodium

●V MAKE IT VEGAN: *Substitute nondairy yogurt.*

# Vegan Blueberry Muffins Ⓥ

*When retooling a recipe to be egg-free, oil and/or fruit purees are often used to provide the moistness eggs typically supply. In this recipe, applesauce plays that role.*

**ACTIVE TIME:** 20 minutes | **TOTAL TIME:** 45 minutes
**MAKES:** 12 muffins

1 cup oats
1 cup all-purpose flour
½ cup whole-wheat flour
½ cup packed brown sugar
2 teaspoons baking powder
½ teaspoon baking soda
½ teaspoon salt
1¼ cups plain soy milk
¼ cup unsweetened applesauce
3 tablespoons canola oil
1 teaspoon vanilla extract
2 cups blueberries
1 teaspoon granulated sugar

1. Preheat oven to 400°F. Line 12-cup muffin pan with paper liners.

2. Place oats in blender and blend until finely ground.

3. In large bowl, combine oats, all-purpose flour, whole-wheat flour, brown sugar, baking powder, baking soda, and salt. In small bowl, with fork, blend soy milk, applesauce, oil, and vanilla; stir into flour mixture until flour is moistened. Fold in blueberries.

4. Spoon batter into muffin-pan cups (cups will be very full). Sprinkle with granulated sugar. Bake until toothpick inserted in center of muffins comes out clean, 23 to 25 minutes. Remove to wire rack; serve warm or cool to serve later.

**EACH MUFFIN:** About 180 calories, 4g protein, 31g carbohydrate, 5g total fat (0.5g saturated), 2g fiber, 0mg cholesterol, 254mg sodium

## IT'S SO GOOD!

A good source of dietary fiber, blueberries are high in vitamin C and manganese, too. They're also just 81 calories per cup, making them a sensible addition to any diet.

# Classic Cheese Omelet

*Simple, versatile, and nutritious, omelets are a great way to start the day. Because the cooking time is so short, you'll need to have your eggs, seasonings, and fillings at the ready so you can give individual attention to each omelet.*

**ACTIVE TIME:** about 2½ minutes per omelet
**TOTAL TIME:** 18 minutes

**MAKES:** 4 omelets

8 large eggs (see Cook's Tip, below)

½ cup water

½ teaspoon salt

½ teaspoon coarsely ground black pepper

2 tablespoons butter or margarine

4 ounces Cheddar, Gruyère, or Fontina cheese, shredded (1 cup)

chopped green onions for garnish

toasted country-style bread (optional)

**1.** Preheat oven to 200°F. Place 4 dinner plates in oven to warm.

**2.** In medium bowl, with fork, beat eggs with water, salt, and pepper 25 to 30 quick strokes to blend mixture without making it fluffy. (Over-beating toughens the proteins in the whites.)

**3.** In 8-inch nonstick skillet, melt 1½ teaspoons butter over medium heat. When butter stops sizzling, pour or ladle ½ cup egg mixture into skillet. After egg mixture begins to set around edges, 25 to 30 seconds, with heat-safe spatula carefully push cooked egg from side of skillet toward center, so uncooked egg can reach bottom of hot skillet. Repeat 8 to 10 times around skillet, tilting as necessary, 1 to 1½ minutes. Cook until omelet is almost set but still creamy and moist on top.

**4.** Position skillet so handle is facing you, and sprinkle ¼ cup cheese on half of omelet. With spatula, fold unfilled half over filling. Shake pan gently to loosen any egg or filling from edge, then slide omelet to edge of skillet. Holding skillet above warm plate, tip skillet so omelet slides onto plate. Keep warm in oven.

**5.** Repeat with remaining butter, egg mixture, and cheese to make 4 omelets in all. Sprinkle with green onions and serve with toast, if desired.

**EACH SERVING:** About 315 calories, 20g protein, 2g carbohydrate, 25g total fat (10g saturated), 0g fiber, 455mg cholesterol, 670mg sodium

## COOK'S TIP

For lighter omelets, substitute four large eggs and eight large egg whites.

# Egg and Black-Bean Burritos

*Scrambled eggs with a sprinkling of Monterey Jack are wrapped in tortillas with black beans and salsa, and it's on the table in 15 minutes!*

**ACTIVE TIME:** 10 minutes | **TOTAL TIME:** 15 minutes
**MAKES:** 4 servings

  1 can (15 to 19 ounces) black beans, rinsed and drained
  1 jar (11 ounces) medium-hot salsa (about 1¼ cups)
  6 large eggs
  ¼ teaspoon salt
  ⅛ teaspoon coarsely ground black pepper
  4 ounces Monterey Jack cheese, shredded (1 cup)
  4 (10-inch) flour tortillas

1. In microwave-safe bowl, mix black beans with salsa; set aside. In medium bowl, with wire whisk or fork, beat eggs, salt, and pepper until blended.

2. Heat nonstick 10-inch skillet over medium heat until hot. Add egg mixture to skillet. As it begins to set around edge, stir lightly with heat-safe rubber spatula or wooden spoon to allow uncooked egg mixture to flow toward side of pan. Continue cooking until edges are set to desired doneness, 4 to 6 minutes. Remove skillet from heat; sprinkle cheese evenly over eggs.

3. Meanwhile, in microwave oven, heat black-bean mixture on High 1 to 2 minutes or until heated through, stirring once. Cover and keep warm. Stack tortillas and place between two damp microwave-safe paper towels; heat tortillas on High 1 minute or until warm.

4. For each burrito, place one-fourth of scrambled eggs down center of tortilla; top with about one-fourth of black-bean mixture. Fold two opposite sides of tortilla over filling, then fold over other sides to form a package.

**EACH BURRITO:** About 575 calories, 28g protein, 71g carbohydrate, 21g total fat (9g saturated), 9g fiber, 344mg cholesterol, 1,550mg sodium

# Chunky Home Fries Ⓥ

*Serve these crispy potatoes with any of the egg dishes in this chapter for an extra hearty breakfast.*

**ACTIVE TIME:** 10 minutes | **TOTAL TIME:** 30 minutes
**MAKES:** 4 side-dish servings

  1½ pounds medium red potatoes
  2 tablespoons olive or vegetable oil
  ½ teaspoon salt

1. Cut potatoes into 1½-inch chunks. In nonstick 12-inch skillet, heat oil over medium heat until hot. Add potatoes and salt and cook until potatoes are golden brown, about 15 minutes, turning them occasionally.

2. Cover skillet and continue cooking until potatoes are fork-tender, about 10 minutes.

**EACH SERVING:** About 180 calories, 3g protein, 27g carbohydrate, 7g total fat (1g saturated), 3g fiber, 0mg cholesterol, 300mg sodium

# Easy Huevos Rancheros

*This hearty one-pan breakfast will perk up your taste buds first thing in the morning. Try it for a light supper with a salad of oranges and greens.*

**ACTIVE TIME:** 5 minutes | **TOTAL TIME:** 8 minutes

**MAKES:** 4 servings

1 ripe medium avocado, peeled and cut into chunks

6 large eggs

¼ cup water

1 tablespoon butter or margarine

1 cup mild salsa

1 can (15 to 19 ounces) black beans, rinsed and drained

¾ cup shredded Mexican cheese blend

8 (6-inch) corn tortillas, warmed

1. In cup, with fork, mash avocado. In medium bowl, with wire whisk, beat eggs and water until well blended.

2. In nonstick 10-inch skillet, melt butter over medium heat. Add egg mixture and cook until eggs just begin to set, 1 to 1½ minutes, stirring constantly with heat-safe spatula or wooden spoon.

3. Spoon salsa over eggs; top with black beans and cheese. Cover and cook until cheese melts and beans are heated through, 2 to 3 minutes longer, but do not stir.

4. Serve egg mixture with tortillas and mashed avocado.

**EACH SERVING:** About 505 calories, 23g protein, 51g carbohydrate, 26g total fat (9g saturated), 13g fiber, 338mg cholesterol, 855mg sodium

# Asparagus-Romano Frittata

*This a great way to use up leftover roasted or grilled asparagus. Just cut the spears into smaller lengths, and heat them briefly in the melted butter before adding the egg mixture.*

**ACTIVE TIME:** 15 minutes | **TOTAL TIME:** 30 minutes
**MAKES:** 6 servings

12 large eggs

¾ cup freshly grated Pecorino Romano cheese

½ cup whole milk

¾ teaspoon salt

⅛ teaspoon ground black pepper

1 tablespoon butter

1 pound asparagus, trimmed and cut into 1-inch pieces

1 bunch green onions, thinly sliced

1. Preheat oven to 375°F. Use a nonstick 12-inch skillet with oven-safe handle, or cover handle with heavy-duty foil for baking in oven later.

2. In large bowl, with wire whisk or fork, beat eggs with Romano, milk, ½ teaspoon salt, and pepper until blended. Set mixture aside.

3. In skillet, melt butter over medium heat. Stir in asparagus and remaining ¼ teaspoon salt; cook 5 minutes. Add green onions; cook 2 minutes, stirring often. Spread vegetable mixture evenly in skillet.

4. Reduce heat to medium-low. Pour egg mixture into skillet; cook, without stirring, until egg mixture sets around edge, 4 to 5 minutes. Place skillet in oven and bake until frittata just sets in center, 9 to 10 minutes.

5. To serve, gently slide frittata out of skillet and onto serving plate; cut into 6 wedges.

**EACH SERVING:** About 235 calories, 18g protein, 5g carbohydrate, 16g total fat (7g saturated), 1g fiber, 443mg cholesterol, 580mg sodium

# Quick Asparagus Crêpes

*For a quick but elegant brunch, dazzle guests with these cream sauce–topped asparagus "crêpes," made from flour tortillas.*

**ACTIVE TIME:** 25 minutes | **TOTAL TIME:** 30 minutes
**MAKES:** 4 servings

2 pounds asparagus
1 tablespoon olive or vegetable oil
2 tablespoons all-purpose flour
1½ cups milk
¼ teaspoon salt
8 (6- or 7-inch) flour tortillas
8 ounces thinly sliced Muenster or Swiss cheese

1. Hold base of each asparagus stalk firmly and bend stalk; end will break off at spot where stalk becomes too tough to eat. Discard tough ends; trim scales if stalks are gritty.

2. In 2-quart saucepan, heat oil over medium heat until hot. Add flour and cook 1 minute, stirring. Gradually stir in milk and salt; bring to boiling over high heat, stirring constantly. Reduce heat to low; simmer 1 minute. Keep sauce warm.

3. In 12-inch skillet, bring ½ inch water to boiling over high heat. Add asparagus, reduce heat to medium-low, and cook until asparagus is tender-crisp, 3 to 5 minutes; drain.

## IT'S SO GOOD!

A single serving of asparagus (one cup cooked) is an excellent source of folate, key to the healthy development of red blood cells and the nervous system, as well as supplying bone-building calcium and vitamin K.

4. Preheat broiler.

5. Top a tortilla with one-eighth of cheese slices, and one-eighth of asparagus spears; roll up. Secure with a toothpick if necessary. Repeat with remaining tortillas, cheese, and asparagus, working quickly so tortillas do not dry out.

6. Place tortilla crêpes on broiler-safe platter; pour sauce over crêpes. With oven rack at closest position to source of heat, broil crêpes until sauce is lightly browned, about 5 minutes. Discard toothpicks and serve.

**EACH SERVING:** About 625 calories, 28g protein, 62g carbohydrate, 30g total fat (14g saturated), 2g fiber, 64mg cholesterol, 1,052mg sodium

# Crustless Leek and Gruyère Quiche

*A quiche without a crust? Don't worry—the delicate custard is so smooth and tasty, you'll never miss the pastry. And did we mention that by losing it, we've saved you 200 calories and 13 grams of fat per serving?*

**ACTIVE TIME:** 20 minutes | **TOTAL TIME:** 50 minutes
**MAKES:** 6 servings

1 pound leeks (about 3 medium)
1 tablespoon olive oil
½ teaspoon salt
6 large eggs
2½ cups whole milk
1 tablespoon cornstarch
¼ teaspoon coarsely ground black pepper
4 ounces Gruyère cheese, shredded (1 cup)

1. Preheat oven to 350°F. Grease 10-inch quiche dish or 9½-inch deep-dish pie plate.

2. Cut off roots and trim dark green tops from leeks. Discard any tough outer leaves. Cut each leek lengthwise in half, then crosswise into ¼-inch-thick slices. Rinse leeks thoroughly in large bowl of cold water, swishing to remove sand. With hands, transfer leeks to colander to drain, leaving sand in bottom of bowl. Repeat process, changing water several times, until all sand is removed. Shake colander several times to remove excess water from leeks.

3. In 12-inch nonstick skillet, heat oil over medium heat 1 minute. Add leeks and ¼ teaspoon salt, and cook until leeks are tender and browned, 12 to 14 minutes, stirring frequently. Transfer leeks to prepared quiche dish and spread evenly over bottom.

4. Meanwhile, in large bowl, with wire whisk, beat eggs with milk, cornstarch, pepper, and remaining ¼ teaspoon salt until well blended.

5. Pour egg mixture over leeks in dish. Sprinkle with Gruyère. Bake until knife inserted in center comes out clean, 30 to 35 minutes. Cool on wire rack for 5 minutes.

**EACH SERVING:** About 260 calories, 16g protein, 11g carbohydrate, 17g total fat (6g saturated), 1g fiber, 247mg cholesterol, 375mg sodium

## IT'S SO GOOD!

Leeks are a source of folate, iron, vitamin C, and bone-building manganese.

# Spinach and Jack Cheese Bread Pudding

*Eat your spinach—for breakfast? This bread pudding bakes up like a cheesy, puffy custard, perfect for brunch or an easy family breakfast.*

**ACTIVE TIME:** 15 minutes
**TOTAL TIME:** 1 hour 15 minutes plus chilling
**MAKES:** 6 servings

6 large eggs

2 cups low-fat milk (1%)

¼ teaspoon dried thyme

¼ teaspoon salt

¼ teaspoon coarsely ground black pepper

pinch ground nutmeg

1 package (10 ounces) frozen chopped spinach, thawed and squeezed dry

4 ounces Monterey Jack cheese, shredded (1 cup)

8 slices firm white bread, cut into ¾-inch pieces

1. Preheat oven to 375°F.

2. In large bowl, with wire whisk, beat eggs with milk, thyme, salt, pepper, and nutmeg until blended. With rubber spatula, stir in spinach, Monterey Jack, and bread. Pour mixture into 13" by 9" ceramic or glass baking dish.

3. Bake bread pudding until browned and puffed and knife inserted in center comes out clean, 20 to 25 minutes.

4. Remove bread pudding from oven; let stand 5 minutes before serving.

**EACH SERVING:** About 280 calories, 17g protein, 22g carbohydrate, 13g total fat (6g saturated), 2g fiber, 233mg cholesterol, 545mg sodium

**MEXICAN-STYLE BREAD PUDDING:** Replace Monterey Jack with *pepper Jack cheese*. Serve with *salsa*.

# Blueberry Pancakes with Warm Blueberry Sauce

*Enjoy a double dose of blueberry goodness.*

**TOTAL TIME:** 30 minutes

**MAKES:** 4 servings

2 tablespoons water

½ teaspoon cornstarch

3½ cups blueberries

5 tablespoons sugar

2 teaspoons fresh lemon juice

1½ cups all-purpose flour

1 tablespoon baking powder

½ teaspoon baking soda

½ teaspoon salt

1¾ cups buttermilk

4 tablespoons butter or margarine, melted

2 large eggs

1. Preheat oven to 250°F. Place cookie sheet in oven.

2. In 1-quart saucepan, combine water, cornstarch, 1½ cups blueberries, and 2 tablespoons sugar, and heat to boiling over medium heat, stirring occasionally. Boil until berries burst, 1 to 2 minutes. Remove from heat; stir in lemon juice.

3. In large bowl, combine flour, baking powder, baking soda, salt, and remaining 3 tablespoons sugar. Stir in buttermilk, melted butter, and eggs just until flour mixture is moistened. Stir in remaining 2 cups berries.

4. Lightly grease griddle or nonstick 12-inch skillet; heat over medium heat until very hot.

5. Drop batter by ¼ cups onto hot griddle, spreading batter gently to make 4-inch rounds. Cook pancakes 2 to 3 minutes. (Pancakes are ready to turn when batter begins to set, bubbles start to burst, and edges look dry.)

6. Turn pancakes over using a wide spatula. Cook 1 to 2 minutes longer, until puffy and undersides are a rich golden brown. Transfer to cookie sheet in oven; keep warm. Repeat with remaining batter, greasing griddle if needed. Serve pancakes with blueberry sauce.

**EACH SERVING:** About 525 calories, 12g protein, 75g carbohydrate, 20g total fat (9g saturated), 5g fiber, 143mg cholesterol, 1,020mg sodium

# Whole-Grain Vegan Pancakes Ⓥ

*These egg-free pancakes provide a double dose of whole-grain goodness.*

**ACTIVE TIME:** 15 minutes | **TOTAL TIME:** 30 minutes
**MAKES:** 12 pancakes, 4 servings

1½ cups plain soy milk
⅔ cup quick-cooking oats
½ cup all-purpose flour
½ cup whole-wheat flour
2 teaspoons baking powder
¼ teaspoon salt
3 tablespoons canola oil

1. Combine soy milk and oats in a medium bowl. Let stand 10 minutes.

2. Meanwhile, in a large bowl, combine all-purpose flour, whole-wheat flour, baking powder, and salt. Stir oil into oat mixture and add oat mixture to dry ingredients. Stir just until flour mixture is moistened (batter will be lumpy).

3. Spray 12-inch nonstick skillet with nonstick cooking spray; heat over medium heat until hot. Making 4 pancakes at a time, pour batter by scant ¼ cups into skillet, spreading batter into 3½-inch circles. Cook until tops are bubbly and edges look dry, 2 to 3 minutes. With a wide spatula, turn pancakes and cook until undersides are golden brown. Transfer pancakes to platter. Cover to keep warm.

4. Repeat with remaining batter, using more cooking spray as needed.

**EACH SERVING:** About 300 calories, 8g protein, 37g carbohydrate, 14g total fat (1g saturated), 4g fiber, 0mg cholesterol, 466mg sodium

# Vegan Pumpkin Waffles Ⓥ

*These warmly spiced waffles are perfect on a crisp fall day.*

**ACTIVE TIME:** 15 minutes | **TOTAL TIME:** 45 minutes
**MAKES:** 18 (4-inch) waffles, 9 servings

⅓ cup quick-cooking oats
1¾ cups plain soy milk
1 (15-ounce) can solid pack (pure) pumpkin
¼ cup packed brown sugar
¼ cup canola oil
1 teaspoon vanilla extract
1¼ cups all-purpose flour
1¼ cups whole-wheat flour
1 tablespoon baking powder
1 teaspoon pumpkin pie spice
¾ teaspoon baking soda
½ teaspoon salt

1. Place oats in blender and blend until finely ground. Add soy milk, pumpkin, brown sugar, oil, and vanilla. Blend until smooth. In a large bowl, mix all-purpose flour, whole-wheat flour, brown sugar, baking powder, pumpkin pie spice, baking soda, and salt. Add pumpkin mixture to dry ingredients and stir just until blended. Set batter aside for 10 minutes.

2. Spray a waffle iron with nonstick spray and preheat. Spoon batter into waffle iron (amount will depend on waffle iron used) and cook according to manufacturers' directions until browned and crisp. Serve while hot and repeat with remaining batter.

**EACH SERVING:** About 385 calories, 10g protein, 60g carbohydrate, 12g total fat (1g saturated fat), 6g fiber, 0g cholesterol, 675g sodium

# Syrupy Banana-Nut Overnight French Toast

*The perfect do-ahead solution for overnight guests or a potluck brunch!*

**ACTIVE TIME:** 20 minutes
**TOTAL TIME:** 65 minutes plus chilling
**MAKES:** 8 servings

- 6 tablespoons butter or margarine
- 1½ cups packed brown sugar
- 5 large ripe bananas, cut diagonally into ½-inch-thick slices; or 3 to 4 very ripe pears or peaches (about 1½ pounds), cored or pitted and sliced; or 1 cup dried cherries, cranberries, or raisins
- 1 long loaf French or Italian bread (12 ounces), cut crosswise into 1-inch-thick slices
- 6 large eggs
- 2 cups milk
- 2 teaspoons vanilla extract
- 1 teaspoon ground cinnamon
- ½ cup sliced almonds or coarsely chopped walnuts or pecans

1. In microwave-safe small bowl, heat butter in microwave oven on High 1 minute or until melted. Stir brown sugar into butter until moistened. With fingertips, press sugar mixture onto bottom of 13" by 9" glass baking dish. (It's OK if mixture does not cover bottom.) Spread fresh or dried fruit over sugar mixture; top with bread slices, cut sides down.

2. In medium bowl, with whisk, beat eggs; whisk in milk, vanilla, and cinnamon. Slowly pour milk mixture over bread; press bread down to absorb egg mixture. Sprinkle with almonds. Cover with plastic wrap and refrigerate at least 2 hours or overnight.

3. Preheat oven to 350°F. Remove plastic wrap from baking dish. Bake until bread is golden brown and knife inserted in center comes out clean, 45 to 50 minutes. Let stand 10 minutes before serving.

**EACH SERVING:** About 570 calories, 13g protein, 89g carbohydrate, 20g total fat (11g saturated), 5g fiber, 191mg cholesterol, 465mg sodium

## IT'S SO GOOD!

A single banana is high in vitamin $B_6$, which is important to the health of our nervous system, as well as key to the synthesis of most of the essential molecules in our bodies. Bananas are also a good source of vitamin C, potassium, and dietary fiber.

# Pizzas, Sandwiches & Burgers

# 2

What's pizza without pepperoni? Can my family give up burgers? And how will we get through lunchtime without deli meats? This chapter provides the answers to these and other questions raised by families reducing or eliminating their meat consumption.

No one will ever miss the meat toppings with our delectable selection of homemade pizzas. Caramelized onions, roasted peppers, and stir-fried broccoli are presented on a range of crust options. Choose bread shells or phyllo, refrigerated dough or from-scratch crusts—whichever pizza base suits your schedule.

We've included a host of tempting sandwich ideas, including some meatless riffs on classic combinations, like Vegetarian Souvlaki and Portobello Cheese "Steak" Wraps. Keep in mind sandwiches and wraps are a great way to mix and match a host of ingredients. Use our recipes as a starting point for your own delicious and healthful combinations. Add a generous pinch of bean sprouts to whatever you're stuffing into a pita bread, for example, and you've added a healthy shot of vitamin C along with a tasty crunch.

And going vegetarian doesn't mean going burgerless—we've included several meat-free versions here, as well as in the chapter "Veggies on the Grill." You'll find they're just as satisfying and substantial without the meat.

*Clockwise from top left: Bulgur Bean Burgers (page 59); Health Club Sandwiches (page 52); Falafel Sandwiches (page 51); Whole-Wheat Pita Pizzas with Vegetables (page 42)*

# Whole-Wheat Pita Pizzas with Vegetables

*We topped whole-wheat pitas with ricotta cheese, garbanzo beans, and sautéed vegetables for a fast dinner the whole family will love.*

**ACTIVE TIME:** 25 minutes | **TOTAL TIME:** 35 minutes

**MAKES:** 4 main-dish servings

- 1 teaspoon olive oil
- 1 medium red onion, sliced
- 2 garlic cloves, crushed with garlic press
- ¼ teaspoon crushed red pepper
- 8 ounces broccoli flowerets (half 16-ounce bag), cut into 1½-inch pieces
- ½ teaspoon salt
- ¼ cup water
- 1 can (15 to 19 ounces) garbanzo beans, rinsed and drained
- 1 cup part-skim ricotta cheese
- 4 (6-inch) whole-wheat pita breads, split horizontally in half
- ½ cup freshly grated Parmesan cheese
- 2 ripe medium plum tomatoes, cut into ½-inch chunks

1. Preheat oven to 450°F.

2. In nonstick 12-inch skillet, heat oil over medium heat until hot. Add onion and cook until golden, 8 to 10 minutes, stirring occasionally. Add garlic and crushed red pepper, and cook 30 seconds, stirring. Add broccoli, ¼ teaspoon salt, and water; heat to boiling. Cover and cook until broccoli is tender-crisp, about 5 minutes.

3. Meanwhile, in small bowl, with potato masher or fork, mash garbanzo beans with ricotta and remaining ¼ teaspoon salt until almost smooth.

4. Arrange pita halves on two large cookie sheets. Bake until lightly toasted, about 3 minutes.

5. Spread bean mixture on toasted pitas. Top with broccoli mixture and sprinkle with Parmesan. Bake until heated through, 7 to 10 minutes longer. Sprinkle with tomatoes to serve.

**EACH SERVING:** About 510 calories, 27g protein, 77g carbohydrate, 13g total fat (6g saturated), 11g fiber, 27mg cholesterol, 1,155mg sodium

# Bistro Pizza

*A winning combination of asparagus, smoked mozzarella, and homemade roasted red peppers brings great flavor to a simple pizza. If thin asparagus is unavailable, use medium asparagus, cutting each stalk lengthwise in half before proceeding with step 4.*

**ACTIVE TIME:** 35 minutes
**TOTAL TIME:** 1 hour plus standing
**MAKES:** 4 main-dish servings

2 medium red peppers (4 to 6 ounces each)

2 cups all-purpose flour

1 package quick-rise yeast

1 teaspoon salt

¾ cup very warm water (120° to 130°F)

2½ teaspoons olive oil

cornmeal

8 ounces thin asparagus, trimmed

6 ounces smoked mozzarella cheese, shredded (1½ cups)

¼ teaspoon coarsely ground black pepper

1. Preheat broiler. Line broiling pan with foil. Cut each pepper lengthwise in half; remove and discard stems and seeds. Place peppers, skin-side up, on foil-lined pan and broil at closest position to source of heat, until skin is charred and blistered, about 10 minutes. Remove from broiler. Wrap foil around peppers and allow to steam at room temperature until cool enough to handle, about 15 minutes. (Wrapping peppers in foil to steam makes it easier to peel off skin.) Turn oven off.

2. Meanwhile, in large bowl, combine flour, yeast, and ¾ teaspoon salt. Add water and 2 teaspoons oil; stir until blended and dough comes away from side of bowl. Knead dough 5 minutes.

3. Sprinkle large cookie sheet with cornmeal. Shape dough into 2 balls; place in diagonally opposite corners of cookie sheet, each 3 inches from edges of sheet. Cover with clean dish towel; let rest 15 minutes.

4. While dough is resting, remove peppers from foil; peel off skin and discard. Cut pepper halves into thin strips; set aside. Cut asparagus stalks into 2-inch pieces. In small bowl, toss asparagus with remaining ½ teaspoon oil and remaining ¼ teaspoon salt.

5. Preheat oven to 425°F.

6. With dough on cookie sheet, pat and stretch 1 ball into a 10-inch round. Bring edge of dough up, folding to make 1-inch rim. Arrange half of cheese, half of red-pepper strips, and half of asparagus on crust. Repeat to make a second pizza. Cover pizzas with clean dish towel and let rest 15 minutes.

7. Bake pizzas on bottom rack of oven until topping is hot and crust is browned and crisp, 25 to 30 minutes. Sprinkle pizzas with black pepper.

**EACH SERVING:** About 395 calories, 17g protein, 52g carbohydrate, 13g total fat (6g saturated), 3g fiber, 33mg cholesterol, 730mg sodium

# Summer Phyllo Pizza

*Using phyllo dough gives this pizza a whole different kind of crunch that you'll love. It's also the perfect stage for thinly sliced sun-ripened tomatoes.*

**ACTIVE TIME:** 15 minutes | **TOTAL TIME:** 35 minutes
**MAKES:** 6 main-dish servings

- 7 sheets (17" by 12" each) fresh or frozen (thawed) phyllo
- 5 tablespoons unsalted butter, melted
- 7 tablespoons freshly grated Parmesan cheese
- 1 cup coarsely shredded mozzarella or crumbled Gorgonzola cheese (4 ounces)
- 1 cup very thinly sliced red onion
- 2 pounds ripe tomatoes (4 large), peeled, seeded, and sliced ¼ inch thick
- 1 teaspoon fresh thyme leaves or ¼ teaspoon dried
- ½ teaspoon dried oregano, crumbled
- thyme sprigs for garnish

## IT'S SO GOOD!

A single serving (one cup) of uncooked tomatoes is an excellent source of vitamin C, which enhances the body's ability to absorb iron. Tomatoes also contain lycopene and other substances associated with lowering the risk of certain cancers.

1. Preheat oven to 375°F.

2. Place phyllo between two sheets of waxed paper, and cover with damp towel to prevent it from drying out. Brush large cookie sheet with melted butter. Lay 1 sheet of phyllo on buttered cookie sheet. Lightly brush top of phyllo with butter. Sprinkle 1 tablespoon Parmesan on top of butter.

3. Lay on another sheet of phyllo, and press so it adheres to first layer. Butter, sprinkle with Parmesan, and layer remaining phyllo sheets in the same way, ending with a sheet of phyllo and reserving the last tablespoon of Parmesan.

4. Sprinkle top sheet of phyllo with mozzarella. Scatter onion evenly over cheese. Arrange tomatoes in single layer over onion. Sprinkle with thyme leaves, oregano, and remaining 1 tablespoon Parmesan.

5. Bake, watching that phyllo only browns and does not burn, 20 to 30 minutes. Garnish with thyme sprigs.

**EACH SERVING:** About 265 calories, 10g protein, 20g carbohydrate, 17g total fat (10g saturated), 2g fiber, 45mg cholesterol, 322mg sodium

# Salad Pizzas

*This pizza is a delightful surprise—a refreshing romaine and red onion salad tossed with a tangy feta dressing and presented on a basil-flavored pizza crust.*

**ACTIVE TIME:** 10 minutes | **TOTAL TIME:** 25 minutes
**MAKES:** 2 main-dish servings

- 1 package (10 ounces) refrigerated pizza dough
- ½ cup loosely packed fresh basil leaves, chopped
- 2 ounces feta cheese, crumbled (½ cup)
- ¼ cup low-fat mayonnaise dressing
- 2 tablespoons low-fat milk (1%)
- ¼ teaspoon coarsely ground black pepper
- 1 small head romaine lettuce (12 ounces)
- 1 small red onion, peeled
- 2 tablespoons freshly grated Parmesan cheese

1. Preheat oven to 425°F.

2. Divide pizza dough in half. On lightly floured surface, with floured rolling pin, roll each half into an 11" by 6" rectangle. Place on greased large cookie sheet. Sprinkle dough with chopped basil and half of feta. Bake until crust is golden brown, 12 to 15 minutes.

3. Meanwhile, in large bowl, using a fork, mix mayonnaise dressing, milk, pepper, and remaining feta.

4. Thinly slice romaine lettuce and onion; add to dressing in bowl. Gently toss until coated with dressing.

5. Pile salad on top of hot pizza crusts; sprinkle with Parmesan and serve.

**EACH SERVING:** About 565 calories, 23g protein, 82g carbohydrate, 15g total fat (6g saturated), 7g fiber, 31mg cholesterol, 1,415mg sodium

## IT'S SO GOOD!

For those of us who grew up on nutritionally deficient iceberg lettuce, romaine is the perfect substitute, providing irresistible crunch *and* good nutrition. Two cups of romaine (which only contains 16 calories) provides more than 100% of the recommended daily value of vitamin K, vital to bone health and blood clotting. It's also high in vitamins A and C, folate, and bone-building manganese, as well as being a good source of the mineral chromium, important to blood-sugar regulation.

# Ricotta-Spinach Calzone

*What a delightfully devious way to get your kids to eat their spinach. Few children can resist the cheesy goodness that is a calzone.*

**ACTIVE TIME:** 10 minutes | **TOTAL TIME:** 30 minutes

**MAKES:** 4 main-dish servings

> 1 package (10 ounces) frozen chopped spinach
>
> 1 cup part-skim ricotta cheese
>
> 4 ounces mozzarella cheese, shredded (1 cup)
>
> 1 tablespoon cornstarch
>
> ½ teaspoon dried oregano
>
> 1 tube (10 ounces) refrigerated pizza-crust dough
>
> ½ cup marinara sauce

1. Preheat oven to 400°F.

2. In small microwave-safe bowl, heat spinach in microwave on High 2 to 3 minutes, just until spinach is mostly thawed but still cool enough to handle. Squeeze spinach to remove excess water.

3. Meanwhile, in small bowl, combine ricotta, mozzarella, cornstarch, and oregano; set aside.

4. Coat large cookie sheet with nonstick cooking spray. Unroll pizza dough on center of cookie sheet. With fingertips, press dough into 14" by 10" rectangle.

5. Sprinkle cheese mixture lengthwise over half of dough, leaving 1-inch border. Spoon marinara sauce over cheese mixture; top with spinach. Fold other half of dough over filling. Pinch edges together to seal.

6. Bake calzone until well browned on top, 20 to 25 minutes. Cut calzone into 4 equal pieces to serve.

**EACH SERVING:** About 400 calories, 21g protein, 43g carbohydrate, 15g total fat (5g saturated), 4g fiber, 19mg cholesterol, 1,055mg sodium

# Mushroom and Cheese Pizza for One

*When the kids are busy with activities and— unbelievably—you find yourself on your own for dinner, here's something tasty you can whip up in just minutes.*

**ACTIVE TIME:** 5 minutes | **TOTAL TIME:** 10 minutes

**MAKES:** 1 main-dish serving

> 1 (6-inch) Italian bread shell
>
> 1 tablespoon bottled spaghetti sauce or pizza sauce
>
> ½ cup shredded Cheddar-and-mozzarella cheese blend
>
> 1½ ounces sliced mushrooms (half a 3-ounce can), drained
>
> ½ teaspoon dried parsley flakes

1. Preheat oven to 450°F.

2. Place bread shell on ungreased cookie sheet. Spread with sauce; sprinkle with ¼ cup cheese. Top with mushrooms, remaining ¼ cup cheese, and parsley.

3. Bake until cheese is melted and bubbly, about 10 minutes.

**EACH SERVING:** About 445 calories, 21g protein, 55g carbohydrate, 17g total fat (9g saturated), 4g fiber, 40mg cholesterol, 1,130mg sodium

# Broccoli-Cheese Polenta Pizza

*Here's a different flavor take on pizza, featuring the toothsome corn goodness of ready-made polenta.*

**ACTIVE TIME:** 20 minutes | **TOTAL TIME:** 25 minutes
**MAKES:** 4 main-dish servings

olive oil nonstick cooking spray
1 log (16 ounces) precooked plain polenta, cut into ¼-inch-thick slices
1 bag (12 ounces) broccoli flowerets
¾ cup part-skim ricotta cheese
¼ cup freshly grated Parmesan cheese
1 teaspoon freshly grated lemon peel
⅛ teaspoon ground black pepper
1 large ripe plum tomato (4 ounces), chopped

1. Preheat broiler.

2. Coat 12-inch pizza pan or large cookie sheet with cooking spray. In center of pizza pan, place 1 slice polenta; arrange remaining slices in 2 concentric circles around first slice, overlapping slightly, to form a 10-inch round. Generously coat polenta with cooking spray. Place pan in oven about 4 inches from source of heat; broil polenta until heated through, about 5 minutes. Do not turn broiler off.

3. Meanwhile, in microwave-safe medium bowl, combine broccoli and *2 tablespoons water*. Cover with plastic wrap, turning back one section to vent. Heat broccoli in microwave oven on High 3 minutes or just until tender. Drain.

4. In small bowl, combine ricotta, Parmesan, lemon peel, and pepper.

5. Arrange broccoli evenly over polenta. Drop cheese mixture by tablespoons over polenta and broccoli; sprinkle with tomato. Broil pizza until topping is hot, 3 to 5 minutes.

**EACH SERVING:** About 200 calories, 12g protein, 25g carbohydrate, 6g total fat (3g saturated), 4g fiber, 18mg cholesterol, 530mg sodium

## IT'S SO GOOD!

Did you know that 1 cup of broccoli contains more vitamin C than 1 medium-size orange? In fact, it provides more than 200% of the daily requirement.

# Vegetarian Souvlaki

*No one will miss the meat in these yummy sandwiches. Make the filling by cutting up your favorite veggie burgers.*

**ACTIVE TIME:** 20 minutes | **TOTAL TIME:** 25 minutes

**MAKES:** 4 sandwiches

- 1 tablespoon olive oil
- 1 large onion (12 ounces), cut in half and thinly sliced
- 4 frozen vegetarian soy burgers (10- to 12-ounce package), cut into 1-inch pieces
- ¼ teaspoon ground black pepper
- ½ teaspoon salt
- 1 cup (8 ounces) plain nonfat yogurt
- 1 English (seedless) cucumber (8 ounces), cut into ¼-inch dice
- 1 teaspoon dried mint
- 1 small garlic clove, crushed with garlic press
- 4 (6- to 7-inch) pita breads, warmed
- 1 ripe medium tomato (6 to 8 ounces), cut into ½-inch dice
- 1 ounce feta cheese, crumbled (¼ cup)

1. In nonstick 12-inch skillet, heat oil over medium heat until hot. Add onion and cook until tender and golden, 12 to 15 minutes, stirring occasionally. Add burger pieces, pepper, and ¼ teaspoon salt, and cook until heated through, about 5 minutes.

2. Meanwhile, in medium bowl, stir yogurt with cucumber, mint, garlic, and remaining ¼ teaspoon salt. Add burger mixture and toss gently to combine.

3. Cut 1-inch slice from each pita to make opening. Reserve cut-off pitas for crumbs another day. Spoon one-fourth of burger mixture into each pita. Sprinkle with tomato and feta.

**EACH SANDWICH:** About 390 calories, 24g protein, 45g carbohydrate, 13g total fat (3g saturated), 6g fiber, 9mg cholesterol, 945mg sodium

**V** **MAKE IT VEGAN:** *Substitute nondairy yogurt and omit the feta.*

## COOK'S TIP

If a recipe calls for an English cucumber and you use a classic cuke with a waxed skin, peel it and discard the seeds if they're bitter. Cut the cucumber in half lengthwise, then, using a teaspoon, scoop out the center by scraping down the length.

# Falafel Sandwiches Ⓥ

*Serve these small, flat bean patties in pita pockets with lettuce, tomatoes, cucumbers, and tangy yogurt. These are vegan if you skip the optional yogurt.*

**ACTIVE TIME:** 10 minutes | **TOTAL TIME:** 25 minutes
**MAKES:** 4 sandwiches

4 green onions, cut into ½-inch pieces

2 garlic cloves, each cut in half

½ cup packed fresh Italian parsley leaves

2 teaspoons dried mint

1 can (15 to 19 ounces) garbanzo beans, rinsed and drained

½ cup plain dried bread crumbs

1 teaspoon ground coriander

1 teaspoons ground cumin

1 teaspoon baking powder

½ teaspoon salt

¼ teaspoon ground red pepper (cayenne)

¼ teaspoon ground allspice

olive oil nonstick cooking spray

4 (6- to 7-inch) whole-wheat pita breads

**ACCOMPANIMENTS:** sliced romaine lettuce, sliced ripe tomatoes, sliced cucumber, sliced red onion, plain low-fat yogurt (optional)

1. In food processor with knife blade attached, finely chop green onions, garlic, parsley, and mint. Add beans, bread crumbs, coriander, cumin, baking powder, salt, ground red pepper, and all-spice, and blend until a coarse puree forms.

2. Shape bean mixture, by scant ½ cups, into eight 3-inch round patties and place on sheet of waxed paper. Coat both sides of patties with cooking spray.

## IT'S SO GOOD!

Garbanzo beans are rich in bone-building manganese, as well as being high in dietary fiber, protein, and iron.

3. Heat nonstick 10-inch skillet over medium heat until hot. Add half of patties and cook until dark golden brown, about 10 minutes, turning them over once. Transfer patties to paper towels to drain. Repeat with remaining patties.

4. Cut off top third of each pita to form a pocket. Place two warm patties in each pita. Serve with choice of accompaniments.

**EACH SANDWICH:** About 365 calories, 14g protein, 68g carbohydrate, 5g total fat (1g saturated), 10g fiber, 0mg cholesterol, 1,015mg sodium

# Health Club Sandwiches ⓥ

*This carrot, sprout, and bean spread combo will delight your palate and satisfy your hunger.*

**TOTAL TIME:** 25 minutes

**MAKES:** 4 sandwiches

- 2 tablespoons olive oil
- 2 teaspoons plus 1 tablespoon fresh lemon juice
- 1 teaspoon honey
- ⅛ teaspoon ground black pepper
- 3 carrots, peeled and shredded (1 cup)
- 2 cups alfalfa sprouts
- 1 garlic clove, finely chopped
- ½ teaspoon ground cumin
- pinch ground red pepper (cayenne)
- 1 can (15 to 19 ounces) garbanzo beans, rinsed and drained
- 1 tablespoon water
- 12 slices multigrain bread, lightly toasted
- 1 large ripe tomato (10 to 12 ounces), thinly sliced
- 1 bunch (4 ounces) watercress, tough stems trimmed

1. In medium bowl, stir 1 tablespoon oil, 2 teaspoons lemon juice, honey, and ground black pepper until mixed. Add carrots and alfalfa sprouts; toss until mixed and evenly coated with dressing.

2. In 2-quart saucepan, heat remaining 1 tablespoon oil over medium heat. Add garlic, cumin, and ground red pepper and cook until very fragrant. Stir in garbanzo beans and remove from heat. Add remaining 1 tablespoon lemon juice and water; mash to a coarse puree.

3. Spread bean mixture on 8 toast slices. Place tomato slices and watercress over 4 slices of garbanzo-topped toast. Top remaining 4 garbanzo-topped slices with alfalfa-sprout mixture and place on watercress-topped bread. Cover with 4 remaining toast slices. Cut sandwiches in half.

**EACH SANDWICH:** About 379 calories, 14g protein, 57g carbohydrate, 12g total fat (2g saturated), 17g fiber, 0mg cholesterol, 545mg sodium

# Fresh Mozzarella and Tomato Sandwiches

*This sandwich is the essence of summer, made with garden tomatoes and our fresh herb sauce.*

**TOTAL TIME:** 15 minutes

**MAKES:** 4 sandwiches

- ½ cup Salsa Verde (see recipe, right)
- 8 slices (½ inch thick) Tuscan bread
- 2 ripe medium tomatoes (6 to 8 ounces each), each cut into 4 slices
- 8 ounces fresh mozzarella cheese, cut into 8 slices

1. Spread about 1 tablespoon Salsa Verde on 1 side of each bread slice.

2. Place 2 tomato slices and 2 mozzarella slices on each of 4 bread slices.

3. Place remaining bread slices, sauce side down, on top. Cut each sandwich in half to serve.

**EACH SANDWICH:** About 455 calories, 17g protein, 38g carbohydrate, 26g total fat (9g saturated), 4g fiber, 44mg cholesterol, 690mg sodium

# Salsa Verde ⓥ

**TOTAL TIME:** 10 minutes

**MAKES:** ¾ cup or 6 servings

- 1 garlic clove, cut in half
- ¼ teaspoon salt
- 2 cups loosely packed fresh Italian parsley leaves
- ⅓ cup olive oil
- 3 tablespoons capers, drained
- 3 tablespoons fresh lemon juice
- 1 teaspoon Dijon mustard
- ⅛ teaspoon ground black pepper

In food processor with knife blade attached, or in blender, combine garlic, salt, parsley, oil, capers, lemon juice, mustard, and pepper. Puree until almost smooth, or blend until finely chopped. If not using sauce right away, cover and refrigerate up to 3 days.

**EACH SERVING:** About 60 calories, 0g protein, 1g carbohydrate, 6g total fat (1g saturated), 0.5g fiber, 0g cholesterol, 140mg sodium

# Portobello Cheese "Steak" Wraps

*A hearty meatless meal, served gyro-style.*

**TOTAL TIME:** 35 minutes

**MAKES:** 4 sandwiches

- 2 medium portobello mushrooms (4 ounces each), stems discarded
- 2 tablespoons olive oil
- 2 medium yellow peppers (4 to 6 ounces each), thinly sliced
- 1 jumbo sweet onion such as Vidalia or Walla Walla (1 pound), thinly sliced
- ½ teaspoon salt
- ¼ teaspoon coarsely ground black pepper
- 2 tablespoons water
- 1 tablespoon balsamic vinegar
- 4 (7-inch) pocketless pita breads
- 8 ounces part-skim mozzarella cheese, shredded (2 cups)

1. Preheat oven to 400°F.

2. Heat nonstick 12-inch skillet over medium heat until hot. Brush both sides of mushrooms using 1 tablespoon oil. Add mushrooms to skillet and cook until tender and lightly browned, about 10 minutes, turning once. Transfer mushrooms to cutting board and cut into ¼-inch-thick slices; set aside.

3. In same skillet, heat remaining 1 tablespoon oil over medium heat until hot. Add yellow peppers, onion, salt, pepper, and water; cook until vegetables are tender and golden, about 15 minutes, stirring frequently. Stir in vinegar; remove skillet from heat. Gently stir in sliced portobellos.

4. Meanwhile, place pitas on large cookie sheet; sprinkle with mozzarella. Heat pitas in oven until cheese melts, about 5 minutes.

5. Roll each pita into a cone; tightly wrap bottom half of each with kitchen parchment or foil to help hold shape and prevent leakage. Fill pita cones with warm mushroom mixture.

**EACH SANDWICH:** About 460 calories, 24g protein, 52g carbohydrate, 18g total fat (7g saturated), 4g fiber, 41mg cholesterol, 1,060mg sodium

## COOK'S TIP

Look for portobello mushrooms with a smooth, fresh appearance and dry surface; refrigerate and use them within several days. To keep portobellos longer, place them in a brown paper bag in the refrigerator or, if packaged, leave them in their tray but remove the plastic wrap and rewrap with paper towels instead.

# BBQ Tofu Sandwiches ⓥ

*Here's a quick and easy way to flavor tofu.*

**ACTIVE TIME:** 20 minutes | **TOTAL TIME:** 25 minutes
**MAKES:** 4 sandwiches

1 package (16 ounces) extra-firm tofu
¼ cup ketchup
2 tablespoons Dijon mustard
2 tablespoons reduced-sodium soy sauce
1 tablespoon molasses
1 tablespoon grated, peeled fresh ginger
⅛ teaspoon ground red pepper (cayenne)
2 garlic cloves, crushed with garlic press
2 teaspoons sesame seeds
8 slices whole-grain bread, toasted
**ACCOMPANIMENTS:** sliced ripe tomatoes, sliced red onion, and lettuce leaves (optional)

## IT'S SO GOOD!

Tofu is a good source not only of protein, but of calcium, omega-3 fatty acids, and antioxidant-activity-promoting copper and selenium. It's also high in iron and sleep-inducing tryptophan.

1. Drain tofu; wrap in clean dish towel. Place wrapped tofu in pie plate; top with a dinner plate. Place 1 to 2 heavy cans on top of plate to weight down tofu to extract excess water; set aside about 15 minutes.

2. Meanwhile, preheat broiler. Coat rack in broiling pan with nonstick cooking spray.

3. In small bowl, combine ketchup, mustard, soy sauce, molasses, ginger, ground red pepper, and garlic, stirring until blended.

4. Remove plate and cans, unwrap tofu, and discard water in pie plate. Place tofu on cutting board with shorter side facing you. Cut tofu lengthwise into 8 slices.

5. Place slices on rack in broiling pan; brush with half of ketchup mixture. Place in broiler about 5 inches from source of heat, and broil tofu until ketchup mixture looks dry, about 3 minutes. With metal spatula, turn slices over; brush with remaining ketchup mixture and sprinkle with sesame seeds. Broil tofu 3 minutes longer.

6. To serve, place 2 tofu slices on 1 slice of toasted bread. Top with tomato, onion, and lettuce, if you like. Top with another slice of bread. Repeat with remaining tofu and bread.

**EACH SANDWICH:** About 230 calories, 14g protein, 35g carbohydrate, 5g total fat (0g saturated), 2g fiber, 0mg cholesterol, 975mg sodium

# Pinto-Bean Burgers ⓥ

*These zesty burgers are a family-friendly solution that gets dinner on the table fast. These are vegan if you skip the optional sour cream.*

**ACTIVE TIME:** 15 minutes | **TOTAL TIME:** 25 minutes
**MAKES:** 4 burgers

- 1 can (15 to 19 ounces) pinto beans, rinsed and drained
- 1 teaspoon ground cumin
- 1 teaspoon minced canned chipotle chile in adobo
- 1 slice pickled jalapeño chile, minced
- 2 tablespoons plus ½ cup mild salsa
- 5 tablespoons plain dried bread crumbs
- 2 tablespoons olive oil
- 4 hamburger buns, warmed
- 4 lettuce leaves
- **ACCOMPANIMENTS:** cilantro leaves, sliced red onion, and sour cream (optional)

1. In medium bowl, with potato masher, mash pinto beans until almost smooth. Stir in cumin, chipotle, jalapeño, 2 tablespoons salsa, and 2 tablespoons bread crumbs until combined.

2. Place remaining 3 tablespoons bread crumbs on sheet of waxed paper. With floured hands, shape bean mixture into four 3-inch-round patties; coat evenly with bread crumbs.

3. In nonstick 12-inch skillet, heat oil over medium heat until hot. Add burgers and cook until lightly browned and heated through, about 8 minutes, turning them over once.

4. Spoon remaining ½ cup salsa on bottom halves of buns; top with lettuce and burgers. Serve with cilantro, red onion, and sour cream, if you like.

**EACH BURGER:** About 350 calories, 11g protein, 51g carbohydrate, 11g total fat (2g saturated), 8g fiber, 0mg cholesterol, 775mg sodium

## COOK'S TIP

To store washed greens, layer the leaves between barely dampened paper towels and place in a perforated plastic vegetable bag (sold next to the sandwich bags in the supermarket) or in a self-sealing plastic bag with a few holes poked in it. (Seal the bag loosely.) Leafy greens should stay fresh in the crisper for up to 5 days.

# Vegetarian Burger with Avocado Salsa Ⓥ

*It's the toppings that make these burgers — start with store-bought vegetarian soy burgers, then turn them into something special with avocado, tomato, lettuce, and alfafa sprouts.*

**TOTAL TIME:** 30 minutes

**MAKES:** 4 burgers

- 1 ripe medium avocado
- 1 green onion, chopped
- 2 tablespoons bottled mild salsa
- 1 teaspoon fresh lemon juice
- 1 tablespoon chopped fresh cilantro
- ¼ teaspoon salt
- 2 packages (6.35 ounces each, 4 burgers total) refrigerated vegetarian soy burgers
- 4 sandwich rolls, split
- 1 large ripe tomato (10 to 12 ounces)
- 4 large lettuce leaves
- 1 cup alfalfa sprouts

1. Preheat broiler.

2. Cut avocado lengthwise in half; remove seed and peel. In small bowl, mash avocado; stir in green onion, salsa, lemon juice, cilantro, and salt.

3. Prepare vegetarian soy burgers as labels direct. Meanwhile, toast sandwich rolls and slice tomato.

4. On 4 dinner plates, arrange lettuce leaves on bottom halves of toasted rolls; top with tomato slices, burgers, and avocado mixture. Replace tops. Serve with alfalfa sprouts.

**EACH BURGER:** About 330 calories, 19g protein, 40g carbohydrate, 12g total fat (2g saturated), 11g fiber, 0mg cholesterol, 738mg sodium

## IT'S SO GOOD!

Avocados contain heart-healthy antioxidants that have been shown to reduce levels of bad (LDL) cholesterol, while elevating good (HDL) cholesterol.

# Bulgur Bean Burgers

*These veggie burgers get their "meaty" texture from a combination of bulgur and black beans.*

**ACTIVE TIME:** 20 minutes | **TOTAL TIME:** 28 minutes

**MAKES:** 4 burgers

> 1 cup water
> ¾ teaspoon salt
> ½ cup bulgur
> 1 can (15 to 19 ounces) reduced-sodium black beans, rinsed and drained
> 1 container (6 ounces) plain low-fat yogurt
> ¼ teaspoon ground allspice
> ¼ teaspoon ground cinnamon
> ¼ teaspoon ground cumin
> ¼ cup packed fresh mint leaves, chopped
> nonstick cooking spray
> ⅛ teaspoon ground black pepper
> ½ cup shredded Kirby (pickling) cucumber (1 small)
> 4 lettuce leaves
> 1 ripe medium tomato (6 to 8 ounces), sliced
> 4 whole-wheat hamburger buns

1. In 1-quart saucepan, heat water and ½ teaspoon salt to boiling over high heat. Stir in bulgur. Reduce heat to low; cover and simmer until water is absorbed, 10 to 12 minutes.

2. Meanwhile, in large bowl, with potato masher or fork, mash beans with 2 tablespoons yogurt until almost smooth. Stir in bulgur, allspice, cinnamon, cumin, and half of mint until combined. With lightly floured hands, shape bean mixture into four 3-inch-round patties. Coat both sides of each patty lightly with cooking spray.

3. Heat nonstick 12-inch skillet over medium heat until hot. Add burgers and cook until lightly browned and heated through, about 8 minutes, turning them over once.

4. While burgers are cooking, prepare yogurt sauce: In small bowl, combine remaining yogurt, remaining mint, remaining ¼ teaspoon salt, and pepper. Makes about 1¼ cups.

5. Divide lettuce, tomato slices, and burgers on bottom halves of buns; add some yogurt sauce and top halves of buns. Serve with remaining yogurt sauce on the side.

**EACH BURGER:** About 295 calories, 16g protein, 58g carbohydrate, 3g total fat (1g saturated), 13g fiber, 3mg cholesterol, 960mg sodium

Ⓥ **MAKE IT VEGAN:** *Substitute nondairy yogurt.*

# 3

# Salad Makes the Meal

In this chapter, we'll show you how salads are a great way to get healthful ingredients into your diet. For example, you may not want to sit down to a pot of beans, but toss a can of cooked beans into your next salad—they add good flavor, substance, and hunger-quieting fiber, plus more protein than any other plant-based food. You may also be surprised to hear that many of the salad greens, like spinach, arugula, and leaf lettuce (but *not* iceberg lettuce), are rich in calcium. Add just 1 cup of broccoli and now you've got more vitamin C than you'd find in an orange.

Many of these recipes are designed to be main-dish salads, with ingredient combinations that are hearty and filling. Add some good crusty bread and these salads will satisfy your dinnertime hunger and sustain you until breakfast rolls around. If we've indicated that a recipe is a side-dish salad, but it sounds really good to you, there's nothing to stop you from enjoying it as the main event of the meal. Depending on the recipe, you can serve it over added greens, or add extra protein to make it a main course.

*Clockwise from top left: Spinach and Nectarine Salad (page 62); Warm Quinoa Salad with Toasted Almonds (page 81); Six-Bean Salad with Tomato Vinaigrette (page 68); Sweet Potato Salad with Lemony Buttermilk Dressing (page 74)*

# Spinach and Nectarine Salad ⓥ

*If you're packing this spinach salad for lunch, toss the nectarines with the dressing and store them separately from the greens. For photo, see page 60.*

**TOTAL TIME:** 15 minutes

**MAKES:** 2 main-dish servings

2 tablespoons orange marmalade
1 large shallot, thinly sliced
2 tablespoons white balsamic vinegar
2 teaspoons olive oil
¼ teaspoon salt
¼ teaspoon ground black pepper
¼ cup slivered almonds
1 package (7 ounces) baby spinach
2 ripe nectarines, pitted and cut into wedges

1. In microwave-safe small bowl or 1-cup liquid measuring cup, combine marmalade and shallot. Cover with vented plastic wrap and cook in microwave oven on High 1 minute. Stir in vinegar, oil, salt, and pepper.

2. In small skillet, cook almonds over medium heat until toasted, about 5 minutes, stirring. Set aside to cool, about 2 minutes.

3. To serve, toss spinach, nectarines, and marmalade mixture until combined. Place on 2 dinner plates; scatter almonds on top.

**EACH SERVING:** About 285 calories, 8g protein, 37g carbohydrate, 14g total fat (1g saturated), 14g fiber, 0mg cholesterol, 420mg sodium

## HOW SAFE IS PREWASHED SALAD?

Packaged greens seem like a perfect shortcut to a healthy meal—until you hear media reports linking them to high bacteria levels or even outbreaks of deadly food-borne illness. Can you really trust the greens without washing them?

Branded, prewashed salad blends sold in hermetically sealed, clear bags are processed with rinse water that contains sanitizing agents such as chlorine. Even this careful process doesn't remove *all* microorganisms, but the bacteria commonly found in bagged lettuce cause food spoilage, not disease. If the salad isn't refrigerated properly or is not eaten before its "use by" date, these bacteria will cause it to turn brown and slimy, alerting you to discard it—before bacteria multiply to unsafe levels. Although bagged blends have an excellent safety record, don't assume all are ready to eat. Always read the small print. Salads from large manufacturers say *washed* and *ready-to-eat* right on the package, but we have found other greens—like watercress, spinach, and shredded cabbage—that looked salad-ready or even had the word *washed* on the front of the bag, but stated *rinse before using* on the back of it.

The truth is, when it comes to foodborne illnesses like E. coli and salmonella, even the most vigorous washing won't help. If the contamination is present, the only thing that will kill it is cooking it to a temperature of 160°F or more.

# Corn and Avocado Salad ⓥ

*The piquant citrus punch of lime and cilantro is the perfect pairing for sweet corn, garden-ripe tomatoes, and avocado. Be sure to use fresh corn cut from the cob when making this in the summer.*

**TOTAL TIME:** 10 minutes

**MAKES:** 4 side-dish servings

- 1 package (10 ounce) frozen whole-kernel corn, thawed
- 1 ripe medium tomato (6 to 8 ounces), cut into ½-inch pieces
- 2 tablespoons chopped fresh cilantro
- 2 tablespoons fresh lime juice
- 1 tablespoon olive oil
- ¼ teaspoon salt
- ¼ teaspoon sugar
- 1 ripe medium avocado
- lettuce leaves (optional)

## COOK'S TIP

To ripen a hard avocado, place it in a brown paper bag with an apple at room temperature; it will ripen in 2 to 5 days. To slow the ripening of an avocado, place it in the refrigerator, where it will ripen in 1 to 2 weeks.

1. In medium bowl, combine corn, tomato, cilantro, lime juice, oil, salt, and sugar.

2. Just before serving, cut avocado in half; remove seed and peel. Cut avocado into ½-inch pieces; toss with corn mixture. Serve on lettuce leaves, if you like.

**EACH SERVING:** About 160 calories, 3g protein, 19g carbohydrate, 9g total fat (1g saturated), 5g fiber, 0mg cholesterol, 196mg sodium

# Six-Bean Salad with Tomato Vinaigrette Ⓥ

*This salad is a tasty powerhouse of protein, iron, bone-building vitamin K, and heart-healthy antioxidants.*

**ACTIVE TIME:** 20 minutes
**TOTAL TIME:** 26 minutes plus chilling
**MAKES:** 18 side-dish servings

1 teaspoon salt

8 ounces green beans, trimmed and cut into 1-inch pieces

8 ounces wax beans, trimmed and cut into 1-inch pieces

1 can (15 to 19 ounces) garbanzo beans

1 can (15 to 19 ounces) black beans or black soybeans

1 can (15 to 19 ounces) red kidney beans

1½ cups (half of 16-ounce bag) frozen shelled green soybeans (edamame), thawed

**TOMATO VINAIGRETTE**

1 small ripe tomato (4 ounces), coarsely chopped

1 small shallot, coarsely chopped

¼ cup olive oil

2 tablespoons red wine vinegar

1 tablespoon Dijon mustard

½ teaspoon salt

¼ teaspoon ground black pepper

1. In 12-inch skillet, heat *1 inch water* with salt to boiling over high heat. Add green and wax beans; return water to a boil. Reduce heat to low; simmer until beans are tender-crisp, 6 to 8 minutes. Drain beans. Rinse with cold running water to stop cooking; drain again. Transfer beans to large serving bowl.

2. While green and wax beans are cooking, rinse and drain garbanzo, black, and kidney beans. Add canned beans and soybeans to bowl with green and wax beans.

3. Prepare Tomato Vinaigrette: In blender, combine tomato, shallot, oil, vinegar, mustard, salt, and pepper. Blend until smooth.

4. Add vinaigrette to beans in bowl. Toss until beans are evenly coated with vinaigrette. Cover and refrigerate at least 1 hour to blend flavors or up to 8 hours.

**EACH SERVING:** About 130 calories, 7g protein, 17g carbohydrate, 4g total fat (0g saturated), 6g fiber, 0mg cholesterol, 230mg sodium

# Vegetables with Sesame Vinaigrette Ⓥ

*This lively mix of green vegetables, cooked just until crisp-tender and tossed with the rich roasted flavor of sesame oil, will have you and your family eating your vegetables every chance you get.*

**ACTIVE TIME:** 25 minutes | **TOTAL TIME:** 30 minutes
**MAKES:** 10 servings

    1 pound asparagus
    2 medium zucchini (8 to 10 ounces each)
    1 medium bunch broccoli
    8 ounces sugar snap peas or snow peas
    1 bunch green onions
    2 tablespoons olive or vegetable oil
    1½ teaspoons salt
    3 tablespoons seasoned rice vinegar
    1 tablespoon Asian sesame oil
    ½ teaspoon sugar

1. Hold base of each asparagus stalk firmly and bend stalk; the end will break off at the spot where stalk becomes too tough to eat. Discard tough ends; trim scales if stalks are gritty. Cut asparagus into 2-inch-long pieces.

2. Cut zucchini into 1½-inch chunks. Cut broccoli into 2½-inch-long pieces. Remove stem and strings along both edges of each pea pod. Cut green onions into 1-inch pieces.

3. In 3-quart saucepan over high heat, bring *1 inch water* to a boil over high heat. Add broccoli and bring back to boiling. Reduce heat to low; cover and simmer until broccoli is just tender-crisp, 4 to 5 minutes. Drain.

4. In nonstick 12-inch skillet, heat 1 tablespoon olive oil over medium heat until hot. Add zucchini, green onions, and ¼ teaspoon salt and cook until vegetables are golden and tender-crisp, stirring frequently; with slotted spoon, remove to bowl.

5. Add remaining 1 tablespoon olive oil to oil remaining in skillet and heat until hot. Add asparagus, snap peas, and ¼ teaspoon salt and cook until vegetables are golden and tender-crisp, stirring frequently.

6. In cup, mix vinegar, sesame oil, sugar, and remaining 1 teaspoon salt. Add zucchini, green onions, and broccoli to vegetables in skillet. Stir in sesame vinaigrette, tossing to coat vegetables well; heat through. Serve vegetables warm, or cover and refrigerate to serve cold later.

**EACH SERVING:** About 85 calories, 3g protein, 10g carbohydrate, 4g total fat (0.5g saturated), 3g fiber, 0mg cholesterol, 465mg sodium

# Barley and Corn Salad Ⓥ

*This fresh summer side dish showcases vegetables that are best at their peak, including fresh corn, tomatoes, and basil.*

**ACTIVE TIME:** 15 minutes | **TOTAL TIME:** 50 minutes
**MAKES:** 12 side-dish servings

2 ½ cups water
1 ¼ cups pearl barley
5 medium ears corn, husks and silk removed
1 small bunch basil
¼ cup rice vinegar
¼ cup olive oil
1 teaspoon salt
¼ teaspoon ground black pepper
2 large ripe tomatoes (10 to 12 ounces each), cut into ½-inch chunks
2 green onions, thinly sliced

1. In 2-quart saucepan, heat water to boiling over high heat. Stir in barley; heat to boiling. Reduce heat to low; cover and simmer 30 to 35 minutes or until barley is tender.

2. Meanwhile, place corn on plate in microwave oven. Cook on High 4 to 5 minutes, turning and rearranging corn halfway through cooking. Cool until easy to handle. Chop enough basil leaves to equal ⅓ cup; reserve remainder for garnish.

3. With sharp knife, cut corn kernels from cobs. In large bowl, with fork, mix vinegar, oil, salt, and pepper; stir in corn, warm barley, tomatoes, green onions, and chopped basil until combined. If not serving right away, cover and refrigerate up to 4 hours. Garnish with basil leaves to serve.

**EACH SERVING:** About 155 calories, 2g protein, 26g carbohydrate, 5g total fat (1g saturated), 5g fiber, 0mg cholesterol, 205mg sodium

# Snap Pea Salad Ⓥ

*This yummy double-pea salad is easy to prepare for company. Use any leftover fresh dill in your next mayonnaise-based salad.*

**ACTIVE TIME:** 10 minutes | **TOTAL TIME:** 15 minutes
**MAKES:** 8 side-dish servings

1 pound sugar snap peas, strings removed
1 package (10 ounces) frozen peas
½ cup minced red onion
2 tablespoons white wine vinegar
2 tablespoons vegetable oil
2 tablespoons chopped fresh dill
1 tablespoon sugar
½ teaspoon salt
¼ teaspoon coarsely ground black pepper

1. In 5- to 6-quart saucepot, heat *2 inches water* to boiling over high heat. Add snap peas and frozen peas; cook 1 minute. Drain vegetables; rinse under cold running water to stop cooking. Drain again; pat dry between layers of paper towels.

2. In large bowl, stir onion, vinegar, oil, dill, sugar, salt, and pepper until mixed. Add peas; toss to coat. If not serving right away, cover and refrigerate up to 4 hours.

**EACH SERVING:** About 100 calories, 4g protein, 13g carbohydrate, 4g total fat (0g saturated), 4g fiber, 0mg cholesterol, 245mg sodium

*Clockwise from left: Barley and Corn Salad, Creamy Two-Potato Salad (page 72), Snap Pea Salad*

# Creamy Two-Potato Salad

*This creamy, mustard-spiked potato salad is made with red and sweet potatoes. It's sure to be a new favorite on the cookout recipe roster.*

**ACTIVE TIME:** 15 minutes | **TOTAL TIME:** 30 minutes

**MAKES:** 8 side-dish servings

  2 pounds red potatoes (8 medium),
    cut into 1-inch chunks

  1 pound sweet potatoes (2 small),
    cut into 1-inch chunks

  ¼ cup red wine vinegar

  1 tablespoon spicy brown mustard

  1¼ teaspoons salt

  ½ teaspoon coarsely ground black pepper

  ½ cup mayonnaise

  ¼ cup whole milk

  2 medium stalks celery, chopped

  1 small red onion, minced

  ⅓ cup loosely packed fresh flat-leaf parsley
    leaves, chopped

1. In 5- to 6-quart saucepot, place red potatoes and enough *water* to cover by 1 inch; heat to boiling over high heat. Reduce heat to low and simmer 2 minutes. Stir in sweet potatoes; heat to boiling over high heat. Reduce heat to low; cover and simmer 8 to 10 minutes or until potatoes are just fork-tender.

2. Meanwhile, in large bowl, with wire whisk, mix vinegar, mustard, salt, and pepper.

3. Drain potatoes well. While hot, add potatoes to dressing in bowl; gently stir with rubber spatula until evenly coated. Let stand until cool.

4. In small bowl, whisk mayonnaise and milk until smooth. Add mayonnaise mixture, celery, onion, and parsley to potato mixture; gently stir with rubber spatula until potatoes are well coated. Serve warm, or cover and refrigerate until ready to serve.

**EACH SERVING:** About 150 calories, 2g protein, 21g carbohydrate, 7g total fat (1g saturated), 2g fiber, 5mg cholesterol, 280mg sodium

## IT'S SO GOOD!

Sweet potatoes are a powerhouse of nutrition. One small baked sweet potato contains more than 250% of the recommended daily value of vitamin A, is a good source of dietary fiber, and is high in vitamin C and manganese, a mineral that supports a lot of important body functions, including bone manufacture.

# Warm Peas and Carrots Salad ⓥ

*This is the perfect salad for kids who love their peas and carrots.*

**TOTAL TIME:** 15 minutes

**MAKES:** 4 side-dish servings

1 cup frozen peas
3 medium carrots, peeled
1 small onion, peeled
1 tablespoon vegetable oil
½ teaspoon salt
1 tablespoon fresh lemon juice
1 head romaine lettuce

1. Place frozen peas in small bowl; cover with boiling water and let stand 5 minutes.

2. Meanwhile, thinly slice carrots and onion. In nonstick 10-inch skillet, heat oil over medium-high heat until hot. Add carrots, onion, and salt, and cook, stirring occasionally, until vegetables are tender and lightly browned.

3. Drain peas; stir into vegetable mixture with lemon juice. Remove skillet from heat.

4. Cut enough lettuce leaves crosswise into ¼-inch-wide strips to measure 4 cups loosely packed; reserve remaining lettuce for use another day. Toss lettuce with carrot mixture to mix well.

**EACH SERVING:** About 96 calories, 3g protein, 14g carbohydrate, 4g total fat (0.5g saturated), 5g fiber, 0mg cholesterol, 350mg sodium

## IT'S SO GOOD!

Containing almost 700 percent of the daily recommended value of vitamin A, one cup raw carrots supports your immune system and vision. Carrots are also a good source of vitamins C and K, dietary fiber, and potassium.

# Sweet Potato Salad with Lemony Buttermilk Dressing

*Here's a new twist on a picnic favorite that you'll turn to again and again.*

**ACTIVE TIME:** 25 minutes
**TOTAL TIME:** 35 minutes plus cooling
**MAKES:** 12 side-dish servings

    3 pounds sweet potatoes (3 large), peeled and cut into 1-inch chunks

    1 lemon

    ⅔ cup buttermilk

    ¼ cup light mayonnaise

    ½ teaspoon salt

    ¼ teaspoon coarsely ground black pepper

    3 stalks celery, thinly sliced

    ¼ cup minced red onion

    ¼ cup loosely packed fresh parsley leaves, chopped

1. In 6-quart saucepot, place sweet potatoes and enough *water* to cover; heat to boiling over high heat. Reduce heat to medium-low; cover and simmer until potatoes are just tender, about 8 minutes.

2. Meanwhile, from lemon, grate 1 teaspoon peel and squeeze 1 tablespoon juice. In large bowl, whisk lemon peel and juice with buttermilk, mayonnaise, salt, and pepper. Stir in celery, onion, and parsley.

3. Drain sweet potatoes; cool 10 minutes. Add to dressing in bowl and gently stir until potatoes are well coated. If not serving right away, spoon potato salad into large container with tight-fitting lid and refrigerate up to 1 day.

**EACH SERVING:** About 130 calories, 2g protein, 26g carbohydrate, 2g total fat (1g saturated), 2g fiber, 2mg cholesterol, 170mg sodium

# Chunky Greek Salad

*This salad is a great big bowl of goodness—pieces of tomato, cucumber, red pepper, olives, and feta tossed with a citrus dressing and a generous handful of refreshing chopped mint.*

**ACTIVE TIME:** 30 minutes

**MAKES:** 12 side-dish servings

2 tablespoons extra-virgin olive oil

2 tablespoons fresh lemon juice

¾ teaspoon salt

½ teaspoon coarsely ground pepper

1 pint grape tomatoes, each cut in half

6 Kirby (pickling) cucumbers (1½ pounds), not peeled, cut into 1" by ½" chunks

1 large red pepper (8 to 10 ounces), cut into 1-inch pieces

1 green onion, thinly sliced

½ cup kalamata olives, pitted and coarsely chopped

¼ cup loosely packed fresh mint leaves, chopped

3 ounces feta cheese (optional), crumbled (¾ cup)

1. In large serving bowl, with fork, combine oil, lemon juice, salt, and black pepper.

2. Add tomatoes, cucumbers, red pepper, green onion, olives, and mint. Toss until mixed and evenly coated with dressing. If not serving right away, cover and refrigerate up to 6 hours. Sprinkle with feta to serve, if you like. Toss before serving.

**EACH SERVING:** About 45 calories, 1g protein, 5g carbohydrate, 3g total fat (0g saturated), 2g fiber, 0mg cholesterol, 195mg sodium

**Ⓥ MAKE IT VEGAN:** *Omit the feta cheese.*

## IT'S SO GOOD!

Olives are high in vitamin E and iron, as well as containing a variety of phytonutrients that help protect cells against the damage caused by free radicals.

# Tofu "Egg" Salad

*Tofu plays a key role in this faux egg salad, absorbing the flavorings and providing the egg-like creaminess. Turmeric contributes its "egg yolk" yellow coloring.*

**TOTAL TIME:** 15 minutes plus chilling

**MAKES:** 4 main-dish servings

    1 package (16 ounces) firm tofu, drained
    ¼ cup mayonnaise
    1 tablespoon sweet pickle relish
    2 teaspoons milk
    ¾ teaspoon Dijon mustard
    ½ teaspoon salt
    ½ teaspoon turmeric
    2 small stalks celery, thinly sliced
    1 head Boston lettuce
    2 small ripe tomatoes (4 ounces each), sliced

**1.** In medium bowl, with fork, mix tofu with mayonnaise, pickle relish, milk, mustard, salt, and turmeric until tofu breaks down into small pieces the size of peas. Stir in celery. Cover and refrigerate to allow flavors to blend or until ready to serve.

**2.** To serve, arrange Boston lettuce leaves and tomato slices on 4 dinner plates; top with tofu mixture.

**EACH SERVING:** About 195 calories, 18g protein, 10g carbohydrate, 11g total fat (1g saturated), 2g fiber, 0mg cholesterol, 445mg sodium

**(V) MAKE IT VEGAN:** *Substitute soy mayonnaise.*

# Tortellini Salad with Peppers and Artichokes

*A hearty salad that's perfect for a potluck.*

**TOTAL TIME:** 30 minutes

**MAKES:** 6 main-dish servings

    2 packages (9 ounces each) refrigerated
      cheese tortellini or 1 package (16 ounces)
      frozen cheese tortellini
    ¼ cup white wine vinegar
    3 tablespoons extra-virgin olive oil
    1 teaspoon sugar
    ½ teaspoon salt
    ¼ teaspoon coarsely ground black pepper
    1 medium red pepper (4 to 6 ounces),
      cut into thin strips
    1 medium yellow pepper (4 to 6 ounces),
      cut into thin strips
    1 ripe medium tomato (6 to 8 ounces),
      seeded and diced
    1 jar (6 ounces) marinated artichoke hearts,
      drained and each cut in half
    2 bunches arugula or watercress, trimmed
      (about 3 cups lightly packed)

**1.** Prepare tortellini as label directs; drain.

**2.** In large bowl, mix vinegar, oil, sugar, salt, and black pepper. Add red and yellow peppers, tomato, artichokes, and tortellini; toss to coat. Cover and refrigerate if not serving right away.

**3.** Just before serving, set aside a few whole arugula leaves for garnish. Tear remaining arugula into bite-size pieces; toss with tortellini mixture. Garnish with arugula leaves.

**EACH SERVING:** About 360 calories, 14g protein, 46g carbohydrate, 14g total fat (3g saturated), 4g fiber, 40mg cholesterol, 555mg sodium

# Pasta, Pepper, and Broccoli Salad Ⓥ

*This salad is a meeting of East and West — enjoy the colors of the Italian flag dressed with a spicy Asian-style vinaigrette.*

**TOTAL TIME:** 45 minutes

**MAKES:** 4 main-dish servings

12 ounces penne or ziti
2 large red peppers (8 to 10 ounces each)
2 bunches broccoli
2 tablespoons olive or vegetable oil
¾ teaspoon salt
¾ cup water
¼ cup soy sauce
1 tablespoon sugar
3 tablespoons Asian sesame oil
3 tablespoons red wine vinegar
½ teaspoon crushed red pepper
2 tablespoons sesame seeds, toasted

1. Prepare pasta as label directs, but do not use salt in water. Drain; keep warm.

2. Meanwhile, cut red peppers into ¼-inch-thick strips. Cut broccoli into 2" by ½" pieces.

3. In 12-inch skillet, heat 1 tablespoon olive oil over medium-high heat until hot. Add pepper strips and ¼ teaspoon salt, and cook until tender-crisp. Remove peppers to bowl. Add remaining 1 tablespoon olive oil to skillet and heat over high heat until hot. Add broccoli and remaining ½ teaspoon salt, and cook until coated with oil, stirring quickly and constantly. Add water. Reduce heat to medium-high; cover and cook 2 minutes. Uncover and cook until tender-crisp, about 5 minutes longer, stirring frequently.

4. In large bowl, mix soy sauce, sugar, sesame oil, vinegar, and crushed red pepper. Add pasta, red peppers, and broccoli; toss to coat. Sprinkle with toasted sesame seeds. Serve warm, or cover and refrigerate to serve cold later.

**EACH SERVING:** About 650 calories, 22g protein, 95g carbohydrate, 22g total fat (3g saturated), 12g fiber, 0mg cholesterol, 1,440mg sodium

# Pasta Salad with Lemon and Peas

*Small shell or bow-tie pasta is dressed in a light, lemony mayonnaise made even more flavorful with the addition of green onions and fresh basil.*

**TOTAL TIME:** 20 minutes

**MAKES:** 16 side-dish servings

- 1 pound bow-tie or small shell pasta
- 1 teaspoon salt
- 1 package (10 ounces) frozen baby peas
- 2 lemons
- 2/3 cup milk
- 1/2 cup light mayonnaise
- 1/4 teaspoon coarsely ground black pepper
- 1 cup loosely packed fresh basil leaves, chopped
- 4 green onions, thinly sliced

1. In large saucepot, cook pasta in boiling salted *water* as label directs, adding peas during last 2 minutes of cooking time. Drain pasta and peas; rinse under cold running water and drain well.

2. Meanwhile, from lemons, grate 1 tablespoon peel and squeeze 3 tablespoons juice. In large bowl, with wire whisk, mix lemon peel and juice with milk, mayonnaise, pepper, basil, green onions, and salt until blended.

3. Add pasta and peas to mayonnaise dressing; toss to coat well. Cover and refrigerate up to 2 days if not serving right away.

**EACH SERVING:** About 155 calories, 5g protein, 25g carbohydrate, 3g total fat (1g saturated), 2g fiber, 4mg cholesterol, 245mg sodium

# Rice Salad with Black Beans Ⓥ

*This is a satisfying meal in one, packed with the zesty flavors of citrus, salsa, and cilantro.*

**TOTAL TIME:** 30 minutes

**MAKES:** 4 side-dish servings

- 3/4 cup long-grain white rice
- 2 large limes
- 2 cans (15 to 19 ounces each) black beans, rinsed and drained
- 1 bunch watercress (4 ounces), tough stems trimmed
- 1/2 cup bottled mild salsa
- 1 cup fresh corn kernels, cut from 2 medium ears of cooked corn
- 1/4 cup packed chopped fresh cilantro
- 1 tablespoon olive oil
- 1/2 teaspoon salt
- 1/4 teaspoon coarsely ground black pepper

1. Prepare rice as label directs. Meanwhile, from limes, grate 1/2 teaspoon peel and squeeze 3 tablespoons juice.

2. In large bowl, mix warm rice, lime peel and juice, beans, watercress, salsa, corn, cilantro, oil, salt, and pepper; toss well. Cover and refrigerate up to 2 days if not serving right away.

**EACH SERVING:** About 405 calories, 24g protein, 81g carbohydrate, 6g total fat (1g saturated), 15g fiber, 0mg cholesterol, 1,125mg sodium

# Sweet and Savory Couscous Salad Ⓥ

*Frozen orange juice concentrate adds zip to the dressing. None in your freezer? You can substitute half regular orange juice and half lemon juice.*

**TOTAL TIME:** 25 minutes

**MAKES:** 6 side-dish servings

1 cup couscous (Moroccan pasta)

1 can (14½ ounces) vegetable broth

¼ cup olive oil

¼ cup frozen orange-juice concentrate, thawed

¼ cup balsamic vinegar

1 tablespoon Dijon mustard

½ teaspoon salt

¼ teaspoon coarsely ground black pepper

2 tablespoons water

1 can (15 to 19 ounces) garbanzo beans, rinsed and drained

3 green onions, chopped

½ cup pitted prunes, chopped

1 small bunch (8 ounces) spinach, tough stems trimmed

2 large navel oranges

¼ cup sliced almonds, toasted (see Cook's Tip, page 63)

**1.** Prepare couscous as label directs, but use broth plus *water* to equal amount of water called for on label; do not use butter or margarine or salt.

**2.** In large bowl, with wire whisk or fork, mix oil, orange-juice concentrate, vinegar, mustard, salt, pepper, and water. Stir in couscous, garbanzo beans, green onions, and prunes; toss well.

**3.** Reserve several small spinach leaves for garnish. Tear remaining leaves into bite-size pieces and stir into couscous mixture. Cut peel and white pith from both oranges. Cut 1 orange into slices; cut each slice in half. Cut remaining orange into bite-size chunks. Stir orange chunks into couscous mixture.

**4.** Spoon couscous salad into large bowl. Garnish with orange slices and reserved spinach leaves. Sprinkle almonds on top.

**EACH SERVING:** About 375 calories, 12g protein, 53g carbohydrate, 14g total fat (2g saturated), 8g fiber, 3mg cholesterol, 825mg sodium

# Main-Dish Wheat-Berry Salad Ⓥ

*This salad serves up a rainbow of goodness—vitamins A, C, B<sub>6</sub>, and K (to name just a few), iron, protein, and antioxidants galore.*

**ACTIVE TIME:** 35 minutes
**TOTAL TIME:** 1 hour 45 minutes
**MAKES:** 4 main-dish servings

1 cup wheat berries (whole-wheat kernels)
1 can (14½ ounces) vegetable broth
1 medium yellow pepper (4 to 6 ounces)
1 small zucchini (6 ounces)
1 small eggplant (1 to 1¼ pounds)
1 package (8 ounces) mushrooms
nonstick cooking spray
2 tablespoons olive oil
1 teaspoon salt
1 teaspoon dried thyme
½ teaspoon coarsely ground black pepper
1 cup frozen peas, thawed
1 small ripe tomato (4 ounces), cut into
  ½-inch chunks

1. In 2-quart saucepan combine wheat berries, broth, and *1¾ cups water* to boiling over high heat. Reduce heat to low; cover and simmer until wheat berries are tender, about 1½ hours.

2. After wheat berries have cooked 1 hour, cut yellow pepper into ¼-inch-wide strips. Cut zucchini lengthwise in half, then cut halves crosswise into ¾-inch-thick chunks. Cut eggplant lengthwise into quarters, then cut each quarter crosswise into ¾-inch-wide slices. Cut each mushroom in half.

3. Preheat broiler. Coat rack in broiling pan with nonstick cooking spray. In medium bowl, mix 1 tablespoon oil, ½ teaspoon salt, ½ teaspoon thyme, and ¼ teaspoon black pepper; add yellow pepper, zucchini, and mushrooms, tossing to coat. Arrange vegetables on rack in broiling pan. Place pan in broiler 5 to 7 inches from source of heat; broil vegetables until tender and browned, 10 to 15 minutes, stirring them occasionally and removing them to large bowl as they are done. Keep vegetables warm.

4. In same medium bowl, mix remaining 1 tablespoon oil, ½ teaspoon salt, ½ teaspoon thyme, and ¼ teaspoon pepper; add eggplant, tossing to coat. Arrange eggplant on rack in broiling pan; broil until tender and browned, 10 to 15 minutes, stirring occasionally. Remove to bowl with other vegetables.

5. About 5 minutes before end of wheat berry cooking time, add thawed peas to heat through. Drain any liquid from wheat berry mixture. Add wheat berries and tomato chunks to bowl with vegetables; toss to mix well.

**EACH SERVING:** About 310 calories, 12g protein, 50g carbohydrate, 9g total fat (1g saturated), 11g fiber, 0mg cholesterol, 1,025mg sodium

# Fruit and Barley Salad Ⓥ

*The simple lime-juice vinaigrette gives this salad its delectable flavor. You can also use mangoes or peaches instead of the nectarines, if you like.*

**ACTIVE TIME:** 15 minutes | **TOTAL TIME:** 50 minutes
**MAKES:** 16 side-dish servings

6 cups water

1 package (16 ounces) pearl barley

2¾ teaspoons salt

4 medium limes

⅓ cup olive oil

1 tablespoon sugar

¾ teaspoon coarsely ground black pepper

1½ pounds ripe nectarines (4 medium), pitted and cut into ½-inch pieces

1 pound ripe tomatoes (2 large), seeded and cut into ½-inch pieces

4 green onions, thinly sliced

½ cup chopped fresh mint

1. In 4-quart saucepan, heat water to boiling over high heat. Add barley and 1½ teaspoons salt; heat to boiling. Reduce heat to low; cover and simmer until barley is tender and liquid is absorbed (barley will have a creamy consistency), 35 to 45 minutes.

2. Meanwhile, from limes, grate 1 tablespoon peel and squeeze ½ cup juice. In large bowl, with wire whisk or fork, mix lime peel and juice, oil, sugar, pepper, and remaining 1¼ teaspoons salt.

3. Rinse barley with cold running water; drain well. Add barley, nectarines, tomatoes, green onions, and mint to lime dressing; with rubber spatula, stir gently to coat. If not serving right away, cover and refrigerate up to 4 hours.

**EACH SERVING:** About 170 calories, 4g protein, 28g carbohydrate, 5g total fat (1g saturated), 0g fiber, 0mg cholesterol, 375mg sodium

## FLAVORFUL FRUIT FIXES

According to the U.S. Department of Agriculture, most Americans are not eating the recommended minimum of 1½ to 2 cups of fruit per day. Here are some speedy ways to add fruit to your diet:

✦ For a punched-up peanut-butter-and-jelly sandwich, add half a banana, sliced.

✦ Drizzle orange or grapefruit segments with honey, then broil until bubbly for a simple winter dessert.

✦ Toss sliced kiwifruit and banana and diced, peeled papaya and pineapple with toasted coconut, lime juice, and sugar for a tropical fruit salad.

✦ To liven up ordinary coleslaw, toss sliced cabbage with halved grapes and chopped, toasted pecans.

✦ Top sliced fresh apples or canned pears with crumbled blue cheese and chopped, toasted walnuts for a European-style dessert.

✦ Ladle plain pancake batter into skillet; top with diced bananas or mixed berries, and cook as usual for a hearty weekend breakfast.

# Chunky Vegetable-Bulgur Salad ⓥ

*Reminiscent of tabbouleh, this bulgur salad also contains cherry tomatoes and two kinds of summer squash.*

**TOTAL TIME:** 20 minutes plus standing

**MAKES:** 8 side-dish servings

2 cups bulgur

2½ cups boiling water

2 lemons

1 tablespoon olive oil

1 small red onion, finely chopped

1 cup cherry tomatoes, each cut in half

1 medium zucchini (8 to 10 ounces), chopped

1 medium yellow summer squash (8 to 10 ounces), chopped

½ cup loosely packed fresh mint leaves, chopped

½ cup loosely packed fresh parsley leaves, chopped

½ teaspoon salt

¼ teaspoon coarsely ground black pepper

1. In large bowl, stir together bulgur and boiling water. Cover and let stand until liquid is absorbed, about 30 minutes.

2. Meanwhile, from lemons, grate 1 teaspoon peel and squeeze ¼ cup juice; set aside.

## IT'S SO GOOD!

We often dismiss parsley as nothing but a bit of color on the plate, but the truth is that just two tablespoons of chopped fresh parsley packs a powerful wallop of nutrition—more than 1,000% of the daily recommended requirement of vitamin K, which protects our bones from osteoporosis and aids in blood clotting, as well as more than 100% of the daily requirement for vitamin C, plus a healthy dose of vitamin A.

3. In nonstick 12-inch skillet, heat oil over medium heat until hot. Add onion and cook until it begins to soften, 5 to 6 minutes. Add tomatoes, zucchini, and squash, and cook until vegetables are tender, 6 to 8 minutes, stirring occasionally.

4. Stir vegetables into bulgur with lemon peel and juice, mint, parsley, salt, and pepper. If not serving right away, transfer to a container with tight-fitting lid and refrigerate up to 1 day.

**EACH SERVING:** About 160 calories, 6g protein, 32g carbohydrate, 2g total fat (0g saturated), 8g fiber, 0mg cholesterol, 160mg sodium

# 4

# Soups, Stews & Chilis

Beans and other legumes are an important part of the vegetarian diet, and the soup pot is where they really shine. They are the most significant source of plant-based protein and supply a host of other important nutrients, so if you're a vegetarian (or responsible for feeding one), it's worth your while to get cozy with these soups, stews, and chilis. You'll find a soul-satisfying selection of bean and lentil recipes made tasty with an exciting array of flavorings, from the comforting spice mixes of India to the chile-spiked pizzazz of Southwestern creations.

Soups are also an easy way to get acquainted with tofu, a source of protein and iron. Tofu is a flavor sponge, making it the perfect healthful addition to any Asian-style broth. We share a variety of recipes, including miso, sweet and sour, and noodle soups.

Our recipes also take full advantage of vitamin-packed seasonal vegetables: from summer peas, tomatoes, and corn to winter squashes and root vegetables. In fact, soups are such a great source of nutrition, think about serving them as part of a larger meal. We've included a number of first-course soups, which are a nice change of pace from the usual dinnertime routine. Whip up a batch, serve it in cups before your main meal, then freeze the rest to serve later on.

*Clockwise from top left: Vegetable-Bean Stew (page 118), Carrot and Apple Soup (page 94); Gazpacho with Cilantro Cream (page 88); Barley Minestrone with Pesto (page 106)*

# Gazpacho with Cilantro Cream

*Recipes for gazpacho abound. This version is topped with a dollop of cilantro-spiked sour cream, a tasty combination.*

**TOTAL TIME:** 30 minutes plus chilling

**MAKES:** 4 cups or 4 first-course servings

    2 medium cucumbers (8 ounces each), peeled

    1 medium yellow pepper (4 to 6 ounces)

    ¼ small red onion

    2 pounds ripe tomatoes (5 medium), peeled, seeded, and chopped

    ½ to 1 small jalapeño chile, seeded

    3 tablespoons fresh lime juice

    2 tablespoons extra-virgin olive oil

    ¾ teaspoon plus ⅛ teaspoon salt

    ¼ cup reduced-fat sour cream or plain low-fat yogurt

    1 tablespoon milk

    4 teaspoons chopped fresh cilantro

1. Coarsely chop half of 1 cucumber, half of the yellow pepper, and all the onion; set aside. Cut remaining cucumbers and yellow pepper into large pieces for pureeing.

2. In blender or food processor with knife blade attached, puree large pieces of cucumber and yellow pepper, tomatoes, jalapeño, lime juice, oil, and ¾ teaspoon salt until smooth. Pour puree into bowl; add coarsely chopped cucumber, yellow pepper, and onion. Cover and refrigerate until well chilled, at least 6 hours and up to overnight.

3. Prepare Cilantro Cream: In small bowl, stir sour cream, milk, cilantro, and remaining ⅛ teaspoon salt until smooth. Cover and refrigerate.

4. To serve, top soup with dollops of Cilantro Cream.

---

**EACH SERVING:** About 156 calories, 4g protein, 17g carbohydrate, 10g total fat (2g saturated), 4g fiber, 6mg cholesterol, 545mg sodium

**V** MAKE IT VEGAN: *Substitute nondairy sour cream or yogurt and soy milk.*

# Quick Gazpacho Ⓥ

*The use of a food processor makes this a snap. Ripe tomatoes are key; for a different look, try yellow tomatoes.*

**TOTAL TIME:** 30 minutes plus chilling

**MAKES:** 8 cups or 8 first-course servings

3 ripe medium tomatoes (1 pound), cut into quarters

1 green pepper, cut into eighths

1 yellow pepper, cut into eighths

1 garlic clove, peeled

2 tablespoons sherry vinegar

2 tablespoons extra-virgin olive oil

1 teaspoon salt

1 teaspoon hot pepper sauce

1 medium cucumber (8 ounces), peeled, seeded, and cut into 2-inch chunks

1 small red onion, cut into eighths

3 cups tomato juice

garlic croutons and sliced fresh basil for garnish

1. In food processor with knife blade attached, blend half of tomatoes and half of each color pepper with garlic, vinegar, oil, salt, and hot pepper sauce until pureed. Pour into large bowl.

2. In same food processor, pulse cucumber and onion with remaining tomatoes and peppers just until chopped. Stir chopped vegetables and tomato juice into pureed vegetables in bowl. Cover and refrigerate until cold, at least 3 hours.

3. To serve, ladle soup into chilled bowls. Garnish with croutons and basil.

**EACH SERVING:** About 75 calories, 2g protein, 11g carbohydrate, 4g total fat (1g saturated), 2g fiber, 0mg cholesterol, 630mg sodium

# No-Cook Avocado and Vegetable Soup Ⓥ

*What a great hot-weather soup when you're famished but have zero desire to turn on the stove. The radishes, veggie juice, chili powder, and vinegar provide spark, tang, and hotness, the celery and cukes freshness and crunch, and the avocados and beans a satisfying creaminess.*

**TOTAL TIME:** 30 minutes plus chilling

**MAKES:** 4 main-dish servings

1 bottle (32 ounces) spicy cocktail vegetable juice

2 large ripe tomatoes (10 to 12 ounces each), seeded and coarsely chopped

2 ripe medium avocados, pitted, peeled, and cut into ¾-inch pieces

1 large stalk celery, thinly sliced

1 medium yellow pepper (4 to 6 ounces), cut into ½-inch pieces

1 medium cucumber (8 ounces), peeled, seeded, and cut into ½-inch pieces

½ bunch radishes, finely chopped

1 can (15 to 19) Great Northern beans, rinsed and drained

¼ cup red wine vinegar

1 teaspoon salt

1½ teaspoons chopped fresh cilantro or ½ teaspoon dried

½ teaspoon chili powder

In large bowl, combine all ingredients. Cover and refrigerate at least 30 minutes or until ready to serve.

**EACH SERVING:** About 290 calories, 12g protein, 45g carbohydrate, 11g total fat (2g saturated), 16g fiber, 0mg cholesterol, 1,555mg sodium

# Cool Cucumber Soup

*Homemade curry oil adds a taste of the tropics to this summer favorite.*

**ACTIVE TIME:** 25 minutes
**TOTAL TIME:** 30 minutes plus chilling
**MAKES:** 4 cups or 4 first-course servings

2 English (seedless) cucumbers (12 ounces each), peeled

1 garlic clove, crushed with garlic press

2 cups (16 ounces) plain low-fat yogurt

½ cup low-fat milk (1%)

1 tablespoon fresh lemon juice

1 ¼ teaspoons salt

2 tablespoons olive oil

½ teaspoon curry powder

½ teaspoon ground cumin

¼ teaspoon crushed red pepper

1 small ripe tomato (4 ounces), chopped

1 tablespoon sliced fresh mint leaves

## IT'S SO GOOD!

If you think cucumbers provide crunch and little else, you'll be happy to know that all those cucumber sticks your kids have been eating contain vitamin C, as well as immune-system-boosting vitamin A, bone-building manganese and magnesium, and potassium, key to healthy muscle and nerve activity.

1. Cut enough cucumber into ¼-inch pieces to equal ½ cup; reserve for garnish. Cut remaining cucumbers into 2-inch pieces. In food processor with knife blade attached or in blender, puree large cucumber pieces, garlic, yogurt, milk, lemon juice, and salt until almost smooth. Pour mixture into medium bowl; cover and refrigerate until cold, at least 2 hours.

2. Meanwhile, prepare curry oil: In small saucepan, heat oil over low heat. Stir in curry powder, cumin, and red pepper; cook until spices are fragrant and oil is hot, about 3 minutes. Remove saucepan from heat; strain curry oil through sieve into cup.

3. In small bowl, combine tomato and reserved cucumber. To serve, stir soup and ladle into bowls. Garnish each with spoonful of cucumber mixture; sprinkle with mint and drizzle with curry oil.

**EACH SERVING:** About 170 calories, 8g protein, 15g carbohydrate, 9g total fat (2g saturated), 1g fiber, 8mg cholesterol, 830mg sodium

# Carrot and Dill Soup

*Combine sweet carrots with fresh orange, dill, and a touch of milk for a refreshing, creamy soup without the cream.*

**ACTIVE TIME:** 25 minutes
**TOTAL TIME:** 1 hour 10 minutes
**MAKES:** 10½ cups or 10 first-course servings

- 1 tablespoon olive oil
- 1 large onion (12 ounces), chopped
- 1 medium stalk celery, chopped
- 2 large oranges
- 2 bags (16 ounces each) carrots, peeled and chopped
- 1 can (14½ ounces) vegetable broth
- 1 tablespoon sugar
- ¾ teaspoon salt
- ¼ teaspoon ground black pepper
- 4 cups water
- 1 cup milk
- ¼ cup chopped fresh dill
- dill sprigs for garnish

**1.** In 5-quart Dutch oven, heat oil over medium-high heat. Add onion and celery; cook until tender and golden, about 15 minutes, stirring occasionally.

**2.** Meanwhile, with vegetable peeler, remove 4 strips of peel (3" by 1" each) from 1 orange, and squeeze 1 cup juice from both oranges.

**3.** Add orange-peel strips to Dutch oven and cook 2 minutes longer, stirring. Add orange juice, carrots, broth, sugar, salt, pepper, and water; heat to boiling over high heat. Reduce heat to low; cover and simmer until carrots are very tender, about 25 minutes.

**4.** Remove strips of orange peel from soup. In blender, with center part of cover removed to allow steam to escape, blend soup in small batches until smooth. Pour pureed soup into large bowl after each batch.

**5.** Return soup to Dutch oven; stir in milk and chopped dill; heat just to simmering over medium heat. Garnish each serving with dill sprigs.

**EACH SERVING:** About 95 calories, 3g protein, 16g carbohydrate, 3g total fat (1g saturated), 3g fiber, 3mg cholesterol, 380mg sodium

**(V) MAKE IT VEGAN:** *Substitute soy milk.*

# Spiced Pumpkin Soup

*This delicious soup gives you a double dose of antioxidant goodness with the combination of pumpkin and carrots.*

**ACTIVE TIME:** 20 minutes  |  **TOTAL TIME:** 45 minutes

**MAKES:** 8 cups or 8 first-course servings

2 tablespoons butter or margarine

1 medium carrot, peeled and finely chopped

1 medium onion, finely chopped

2 garlic cloves, minced

2 teaspoons ground cumin

½ teaspoon ground cinnamon

1 carton (32 ounces) vegetable broth

1 can (29 ounces) solid pack pumpkin (not pumpkin-pie mix)

1 can (12 ounces) carrot juice

½ cup pumpkin seeds (pepitas), roasted and shelled

## COOK'S TIP

If you can't find roasted pumpkin seeds in your supermarket, roast them yourself: In a 10-inch skillet, toast pumpkin seeds over medium heat until lightly browned, stirring frequently.

1. In 4-quart saucepan, melt butter over medium heat. Add carrot and onion; cook until soft, 8 to 10 minutes, stirring frequently. Add garlic, cumin, and cinnamon; cook 1 minute, stirring. Add broth, pumpkin, and carrot juice to saucepan, stirring to combine. Cover and heat to boiling over high heat. Reduce heat to low; cover and simmer, 15 minutes to blend flavors.

2. Stir soup just before serving. Pass pumpkin seeds to sprinkle over soup.

**EACH SERVING:** About 190 calories, 8g protein, 20g carbohydrate, 10g total fat (2g saturated), 5g fiber, 0mg cholesterol, 660mg sodium

# Onion Soup with Parmesan Croutons

*For the richest flavor, be sure to slow-cook the leeks, shallots, and onions until they are tender, sweet, and golden brown—don't rush!*

**ACTIVE TIME:** 55 minutes
**TOTAL TIME:** 1 hour 50 minutes
**MAKES:** 10 cups or 10 first-course servings

1 bunch (1 pound) leeks

2 tablespoons butter or margarine

1 tablespoon olive oil

3 large onions (12 ounces each), each cut in half and thinly sliced

4 large shallots, each cut in half and thinly sliced

pinch dried thyme

2 tablespoons brandy

3 cans (14¼ ounces each) vegetable broth

1 teaspoon salt

¼ teaspoon coarsely ground black pepper

4 cups water

4 ounces French bread, cut diagonally into ten ¾-inch-thick slices

¼ cup coarsely grated Parmesan cheese

1. Cut off roots and leaf ends from leeks. Discard any tough outer leaves. Cut each leek lengthwise in half, then crosswise into ¼-inch-thick slices. Place leeks in large bowl of *cold water*; with hand, swish them around to remove any sand. Transfer leeks to colander. Repeat process, changing water several times, until all sand is removed. Drain well.

2. In 8-quart saucepot, heat butter and oil over medium-high heat until butter melts. Add leeks, onions, shallots, and thyme, cover, and cook until tender and deep golden brown, 40 to 45 minutes, stirring occasionally.

3. Remove cover and increase heat to high. Add brandy and cook 1 minute, stirring and scraping bottom of saucepot. Add broth, salt, pepper, and water; heat to boiling over high heat. Reduce heat to low; cover and simmer 20 minutes.

4. Meanwhile, preheat oven to 450°F. Place bread slices in 15½" by 10½" jelly-roll pan or on large baking sheet; bake 3 minutes. Turn slices over and sprinkle tops with Parmesan; bake until croutons are toasted, about 5 minutes longer. Top each serving of soup with a Parmesan crouton.

**EACH SERVING:** About 135 calories, 6g protein, 16g carbohydrate, 5g total fat (1g saturated), 2g fiber, 2mg cholesterol, 770mg sodium

## COOK'S TIP

The croutons can be made up to two days ahead and stored in an airtight container; the soup reheats nicely if made the day before serving.

# Cauliflower-Cheddar Soup

*This is so rich, your guests won't believe it's made with milk instead of cream. Use a blender — not a food processor — to puree the soup for an extra-smooth texture.*

**ACTIVE TIME:** 25 minutes | **TOTAL TIME:** 1 hour
**MAKES:** 9 cups or 8 first-course serings

2 tablespoons butter or margarine

1 medium onion, chopped

¼ cup all-purpose flour

½ teaspoon salt

2 cups milk

1 can (14½ ounces) vegetable broth

1½ cups water

1 head cauliflower (2½ pounds), cut into 1-inch chunks

1 teaspoon Dijon mustard

8 ounces sharp Cheddar cheese, shredded (2 cups)

1. In 4-quart saucepan, melt butter over medium heat. Add onion and cook until tender and golden, about 10 minutes, stirring occasionally. Stir in flour and salt; cook 2 minutes, stirring frequently. Gradually stir in milk, broth, and water; add cauliflower and heat to boiling over high heat. Reduce heat to low; cover and simmer until cauliflower is tender, about 10 minutes.

2. In blender, with center part of cover removed to allow steam to escape, blend cauliflower mixture at low speed in small batches until very smooth.

3. Return cauliflower mixture to saucepan; heat over medium heat until hot, stirring occasionally. Remove from heat; add mustard and 1½ cups Cheddar, stirring until melted and smooth. Garnish soup with remaining ½ cup Cheddar to serve.

**EACH SERVING:** About 230 calories, 13g protein, 14g carbohydrate, 15g total fat (8g saturated), 2g fiber, 41mg cholesterol, 575mg sodium

## COOK'S TIP

Make this soup a day or two ahead and reheat on low just before serving. Don't let it boil or the cheese may get stringy.

# Red Lentil and Vegetable Soup Ⓥ

*This meal-in-a-bowl brims with fill-you-up soluble fiber, thanks to the lentils. Translation: It may help keep weight down and lower total and "bad" LDL cholesterol. The lentils, spinach, and tomatoes, all rich in potassium, work to keep blood pressure in check, too.*

**ACTIVE TIME:** 20 minutes | **TOTAL TIME:** 30 minutes
**MAKES:** 4 main-dish servings

- 1 tablespoon olive oil
- 4 medium carrots, peeled and chopped
- 1 small onion, chopped
- 1 teaspoon ground cumin
- 1 can (14½ ounces) diced tomatoes
- 1 cup red lentils, rinsed and picked through (see Cook's Tip, right)
- 1 can (14½ ounces) vegetable broth
- 2 cups water
- ¼ teaspoon salt
- ⅛ teaspoon ground black pepper
- 1 bag (5 ounces) baby spinach

1. In 4-quart saucepan, heat oil over medium heat until hot. Add carrots and onion, and cook until tender and lightly browned, 6 to 8 minutes. Stir in cumin; cook 1 minute.

2. Add tomatoes with their juice, lentils, broth, water, salt, and pepper; cover and heat to boiling over high heat. Reduce heat to low; cover and simmer until lentils are tender, 8 to 10 minutes.

3. Just before serving, stir in spinach.

**EACH SERVING:** About 265 calories, 16g protein, 41g carbohydrate, 5g total fat (1g saturated), 13g fiber, 0mg cholesterol, 645mg sodium

## COOK'S TIP

If you can't find red lentils, feel free to substitute another color. The cooking time might be just a bit longer, as red lentils tend to cook faster than other types of lentils.

# Lentil and Macaroni Soup Ⓥ

*This flavorful and filling soup, chock-full of vegetables, lentils, and pasta, needs only some crusty bread to become a meal. And there's enough to enjoy another day. This is vegan if you skip the optional Parmesan.*

**ACTIVE TIME:** 25 minutes | **TOTAL TIME:** 55 minutes

**MAKES:** 6 main-dish servings

- 1 tablespoon olive oil
- 2 medium carrots, peeled and cut into ¼-inch dice
- 1 medium onion, chopped
- 2 garlic cloves, crushed with garlic press
- 1 can (14½ ounces) tomatoes in puree
- 1 can (14½ ounces) vegetable broth
- ¾ cup lentils, rinsed and picked through
- ½ teaspoon salt
- ½ teaspoon coarsely ground black pepper
- ¼ teaspoon dried thyme
- 6 cups water
- 1 bunch (1 pound) Swiss chard, trimmed and coarsely chopped
- ¾ cup elbow macaroni
- 1 cup fresh basil leaves, chopped
- freshly grated Parmesan cheese (optional)

1. In nonstick 5- to 6-quart Dutch oven, heat oil over medium heat until hot. Add carrots, onion, and garlic, and cook until vegetables are tender and golden, about 10 minutes, stirring occasionally. Add tomatoes with their puree, broth, lentils, salt, pepper, thyme, and water; heat to boiling over high heat, stirring to break up tomatoes with side of spoon. Reduce heat to low; cover and simmer until lentils are almost tender, about 20 minutes.

2. Stir in Swiss chard and macaroni; heat to boiling over medium-high heat. Reduce heat to medium; cook until macaroni is tender, about 10 minutes. Stir in basil. Serve sprinkled with Parmesan, if you like.

**EACH SERVING:** About 200 calories, 12g protein, 34g carbohydrate, 3g total fat (0g saturated), 10g fiber, 0mg cholesterol, 810mg sodium

## IT'S SO GOOD!

Swiss chard is a great addition to the vegetarian diet. It's high in vitamin K, potassium, manganese, and magnesium, all of which promote bone health, as well as being a good source of calcium. It's also high in immune system-boosting vitamins A (more than 100% of the recommended daily value) and C and iron.

# Lentil Soup with Tubettini

*This soup is so hearty and satisfying—the perfect antidote to a cold winter's day. Top with some cheese, if you like, or a drizzle of flavorful olive oil.*

**ACTIVE TIME:** 20 minutes | **TOTAL TIME:** 50 minutes
**MAKES:** 6 main-dish servings

2 tablespoons olive oil

2 medium carrots, peeled and diced

1 medium onion, chopped

2 garlic cloves, minced

1 can (16 ounces) tomatoes in puree

1 can (14½ ounces) vegetable broth

¾ cup lentils, rinsed and picked through

½ teaspoon salt

½ teaspoon coarsely ground black pepper

½ teaspoon dried thyme

6 cups water

½ small (10-ounce) head escarole, torn into 2-inch pieces (4 cups firmly packed)

¼ package (16-ounce) tubettini pasta

¾ cup freshly grated Parmesan cheese (optional)

1. In 5-quart Dutch oven or saucepot, heat oil over medium-high heat until hot. Add carrots, onion, and garlic, and cook until onion is until tender and golden, about 10 minutes. Add tomatoes with their puree, broth, lentils, salt, pepper, thyme, and water; heat to boiling over high heat, stirring to break up tomatoes. Reduce heat to low; cover and simmer until lentils are almost tender, about 20 minutes.

2. Stir in escarole and tubettini; heat to boiling over high heat. Reduce heat to medium; cook until tubettini is tender, about 10 minutes. Sprinkle with Parmesan to serve, if you like.

**EACH SERVING:** About 260 calories, 12g protein, 42g carbohydrate, 6g total fat (1g saturated), 8g fiber, 0mg cholesterol, 345mg sodium

 **V** MAKE IT VEGAN: *Omit the Parmesan.*

# Curried Lentil Soup

*Based on an Indian classic, this recipe is bound to become a staple in your soup-making repertoire. Lentils, unlike other dried legumes, don't require presoaking, so this can be prepared in less time than most other bean soups. Serve with toasted whole-wheat pita breads.*

**ACTIVE TIME:** 30 minutes
**TOTAL TIME:** 1 hour 25 minutes
**MAKES:** 5 main-dish servings

2 tablespoons vegetable oil

4 carrots, peeled and finely chopped

2 large stalks celery, finely chopped

1 large onion (12 ounces), finely chopped

1 medium Granny Smith apple, peeled, cored, and finely chopped

1 tablespoon grated, peeled fresh ginger

1 large garlic clove, crushed with garlic press

2 teaspoons curry powder

¾ teaspoon ground cumin

¾ teaspoon ground coriander

1 package (16 ounces) lentils, rinsed and picked through

5 cups water

2 cans (14½ ounces each) vegetable broth

¼ cup chopped fresh cilantro

½ teaspoon salt

plain low-fat yogurt

1. In 5-quart Dutch oven, heat oil over medium-high heat until hot. Add carrots, celery, onion, and apple; cook until lightly browned, 10 to 15 minutes, stirring occasionally. Add ginger, garlic, curry powder, cumin, and coriander; cook, stirring, 1 minute. Add lentils, water, and broth; heat to boiling over high heat. Reduce heat; cover and simmer until lentils are tender, 45 to 55 minutes, stirring occasionally.

2. Stir in cilantro and salt. To serve, top soup with dollops of yogurt.

**EACH SERVING:** About 434 calories, 27g protein, 69g carbohydrate, 7g total fat (1g saturated), 25g fiber, 0mg cholesterol, 966mg sodium

Ⓥ  MAKE IT VEGAN: *Substitute nondairy yogurt.*

# Summer Garden Soup ⓥ

*We incorporate a cornucopia of ripe summer vegetables into this healthy, easy-to-make soup. Serve with our Grilled Three-Cheese Sandwiches (page 201). One half sandwich plus a serving of soup makes a hearty meal.*

**ACTIVE TIME:** 15 minutes | **TOTAL TIME:** 50 minutes
**MAKES:** 9 main-dish servings

- 2 tablespoons olive oil
- 1 large onion (12 ounces), chopped
- 3 cups water
- 3 medium zucchini and/or yellow summer squashes (8 to 10 ounces each), coarsely chopped
- 2 red and/or yellow peppers, coarsely chopped
- 3 large ripe tomatoes (10 to 12 ounces each), chopped
- 3 garlic cloves, crushed with garlic press
- ½ teaspoon fennel seeds
- 2 teaspoons salt
- ¼ teaspoon ground black pepper
- sliced fresh basil leaves for garnish

1. In 5-quart saucepot, heat oil over medium-high heat until hot. Add onion; cook until tender and lightly browned, about 10 minutes. Add water, zucchini, peppers, tomatoes, garlic, fennel seeds, salt, and black pepper; heat to boiling over high heat. Reduce heat to medium; cook until vegetables are tender, about 20 minutes.

2. Remove 4 cups soup from saucepot. In blender, with center part of cover removed to allow steam to escape, blend the 4 cups soup, in small batches, until smooth. Return pureed soup to saucepot. Reheat soup to serve hot, or refrigerate to serve cold later. Garnish with basil.

**EACH SERVING:** About 120 calories, 4g protein, 18g carbohydrate, 5g total fat (1g saturated), 5g fiber, 0mg cholesterol, 795mg sodium

## IT'S SO GOOD!

A recent study has shown that crushed fresh garlic is more effective in supporting cardiovascular health than pre-peeled garlic from a jar. That means, over time, just a few extra minutes of prep could improve your family's health!

# Not Your Grandma's Vegetable Soup ⓥ

*It's impossible to peel beets without getting red all over your hands—unless you wear rubber gloves. For easy cleanup, always peel beets in the sink. This is vegan if you skip the optional sour cream.*

**ACTIVE TIME:** 15 minutes
**TOTAL TIME:** 1 hour 15 minutes
**MAKES:** 5 main-dish servings

1 tablespoon olive oil
1 medium onion, chopped
1 garlic clove, crushed with garlic press
½ teaspoon ground allspice
1 can (14½ ounces) diced tomatoes
1 pound (not including tops) beets
6 cups sliced green cabbage (1 pound)
3 large carrots, peeled and cut into
   ½-inch chunks
4 cups water
1 can (14½ ounces) vegetable broth
1 bay leaf
¾ teaspoon salt
2 tablespoons red wine vinegar
¼ cup loosely packed fresh dill or parsley
   leaves, chopped
reduced-fat sour cream (optional)

1. In 5- to 6-quart saucepot, heat oil over medium heat until hot. Add onion and cook until tender, about 8 minutes. Stir in garlic and allspice; cook 30 seconds. Add tomatoes with their juice and cook 5 minutes.

## IT'S SO GOOD!

Want your kids to eat beets? Try slipping these sweet-tasting root vegetables into salads or a soup like this one. A single serving (one cup cooked beets) is an excellent source of folate, which plays a vital role in the proper development of red blood cells, as well as supporting healthy nervous system function. It is also a very good source of potassium and bone-building manganese.

2. Meanwhile, peel beets and shred in food processor (or on the coarse side of box grater).

3. Add beets to onion mixture along with cabbage, carrots, water, broth, bay leaf, and salt; heat to boiling over high heat. Reduce heat to medium-low; cover and simmer until all vegetables are tender, about 30 minutes.

4. Remove bay leaf. Stir in vinegar and dill. Serve with sour cream, if you like.

**EACH SERVING:** About 160 calories, 5g protein, 27g carbohydrate, 5g total fat (1g saturated), 6g fiber, 5mg cholesterol, 920mg sodium

# Tomato, Escarole, and Tortellini Soup

*You can make this healthy and soul-satisfying soup from scratch in almost the same amount of time it would take you to heat up a frozen pizza in the oven.*

**ACTIVE TIME:** 10 minutes | **TOTAL TIME:** 20 minutes

**MAKES:** 4 main-dish servings

- 1 package (9 ounces) fresh cheese tortellini or mini ravioli
- 2 teaspoons olive oil
- 2 stalks celery, thinly sliced
- ½ medium (12- to 14-ounce) head escarole, cut into bite-size pieces (5 cups)
- 1 can (14½ ounces) diced tomatoes with sweet onions
- 1 can (14½ ounces) vegetable broth
- 1 cup water
- 4 tablespoons freshly grated Romano cheese

**1.** In 3-quart saucepan, cook tortellini as label directs.

**2.** Meanwhile, in 4-quart saucepan, heat oil over medium heat until hot. Add celery and cook until tender-crisp, about 5 minutes, stirring occasionally. Stir in escarole, tomatoes, broth, and water. Cover and heat to boiling over high heat. Remove saucepan from heat.

**3.** Drain tortellini; gently stir into soup. Divide soup evenly among four large bowls; sprinkle each serving with 1 tablespoon Romano.

**EACH SERVING:** About 200 calories, 10g protein, 25g carbohydrate, 7g total fat (3g saturated), 5g fiber, 14mg cholesterol, 1,185mg sodium

# Barley Minestrone with Pesto

*Top this soup with a dollop of our homemade pesto, which you can make in a mini food processor. No mini processor? Store-bought refrigerated pesto makes an excellent stand-in— although it's not as light as our version.*

**ACTIVE TIME:** 50 minutes
**TOTAL TIME:** 1 hour 15 minutes

**MAKES:** 6 main-dish servings

### MINESTRONE

- 1 cup pearl barley
- 1 tablespoon olive oil
- 2 cups thinly sliced green cabbage (about ¼ small head)
- 2 large carrots, peeled, each cut lengthwise in half, then crosswise into ½-inch-thick slices
- 2 large stalks celery, cut into ½-inch dice
- 1 medium onion, cut into ½-inch dice
- 1 garlic clove, finely chopped
- 3 cups water
- 2 cans (14½ ounces each) vegetable broth
- 1 can (14½ ounces) diced tomatoes
- ¼ teaspoon salt
- 1 medium zucchini (8 to 10 ounces), cut into ½-inch dice
- 4 ounces green beans, trimmed and cut into ½-inch pieces (1 cup)

### LIGHT PESTO

- 1 cup firmly packed fresh basil leaves
- 2 tablespoons olive oil
- 2 tablespoons water
- ¼ teaspoon salt
- ¼ cup freshly grated Romano cheese
- 1 garlic clove, finely chopped

**1.** Prepare Minestrone: Heat 5- to 6-quart Dutch oven over medium-high heat until hot. Add barley and cook until toasted and fragrant, 3 to 4 minutes, stirring constantly. Transfer barley to small bowl; set aside.

**2.** In same Dutch oven, heat oil over medium-high heat until hot. Add cabbage, carrots, celery, and onion; cook until vegetables are tender and lightly browned, 8 to 10 minutes, stirring occasionally. Add garlic and cook until fragrant, 30 seconds. Stir in barley, water, broth, tomatoes with their juice, and salt. Cover and heat to boiling over high heat. Reduce heat to low and simmer 25 minutes.

**3.** Stir zucchini and green beans into barley mixture; increase heat to medium, cover, and cook until all vegetables are barely tender, 10 to 15 minutes longer.

**4.** Meanwhile, prepare Light Pesto: In blender container with narrow base or in mini food processor, combine basil, oil, water, and salt; cover and blend until mixture is pureed. Transfer pesto to small bowl; stir in Romano and garlic. Makes about ½ cup pesto.

**5.** Ladle minestrone into 6 large soup bowls. Top each serving with some pesto.

**EACH SERVING SOUP:** About 215 calories, 7g protein, 42g carbohydrate, 4g total fat (0g saturated), 9g fiber, 0mg cholesterol, 690mg sodium

**EACH TEASPOON PESTO:** About 15 calories, 0g protein, 0g carbohydrate, 1g total fat (0g saturated), 0g fiber, 1mg cholesterol, 35mg sodium

# Hot and Sour Soup

*We streamlined the seasonings to help get this popular Asian soup on the table in record time — without sacrificing the great taste.*

**ACTIVE TIME:** 15 minutes | **TOTAL TIME:** 30 minutes

**MAKES:** 4 main-dish servings

1 tablespoon vegetable oil

4 ounces shiitake mushrooms, stems discarded and caps thinly sliced

3 tablespoons reduced-sodium soy sauce

1 package (16 ounces) extra-firm tofu, drained, patted dry, and cut into 1-inch cubes

2 tablespoons cornstarch

1 cup water

1 carton (32 ounces) vegetable broth

3 tablespoons seasoned rice vinegar

2 tablespoons grated, peeled fresh ginger

½ teaspoon Asian sesame oil

¼ teaspoon ground red pepper (cayenne)

2 large eggs, beaten

2 green onions, thinly sliced

1. In 5-quart saucepot, heat vegetable oil over medium-high heat until hot. Add mushrooms, soy sauce, and tofu, and cook until liquid evaporates, about 5 minutes, gently stirring often.

2. In cup, with fork, mix cornstarch with ¼ cup water until cornstarch is dissolved; set aside. Add broth and remaining ¾ cup water to tofu mixture; heat to boiling over high heat. Stir in cornstarch mixture and boil 30 seconds, stirring. Reduce heat to medium-low; stir in vinegar, ginger, sesame oil, and red pepper, and simmer 5 minutes.

3. Remove saucepot from heat. Slowly pour beaten eggs into soup in a thin, steady stream around the edge of the saucepot. Carefully stir the soup once in a circular motion so eggs separate into strands. Serve sprinkled with green onions.

**EACH SERVING:** About 235 calories, 15g protein, 16g carbohydrate, 13g total fat (2g saturated), 2g fiber, 106mg cholesterol, 1,847mg sodium

## IT'S SO GOOD!

Shiitake mushrooms are a good source of iron, as well as vitamin C (which increases the absorption rate of the iron), protein, and heart-healthy dietary fiber.

# Asian-Style Corn Chowder

*Here's a deliciously different spin on the American classic. You can find lemongrass and chili paste in Thai food markets, though lemongrass is now showing up in the produce section of some large supermarkets and chili paste can often be found in the Asian food section.*

**ACTIVE TIME:** 20 minutes | **TOTAL TIME:** 30 minutes
**MAKES:** 9½ cups or 10 first-course servings

2 tablespoons butter or margarine

2 tablespoons minced, peeled fresh ginger

2 medium shallots

2 medium garlic cloves, minced

1 medium onion, diced

1 stalk (12 inches long) fresh lemongrass, lightly pounded and then cut into 4-inch-long pieces, or 3 strips lemon peel (3" by 1" each)

2 cans (14½ ounces each) vegetable broth

1 bag (20 ounces) frozen whole-kernel corn, thawed

1½ teaspoons sugar

½ teaspoon salt

2 cups water

½ cup half-and-half or light cream

chopped fresh cilantro leaves for garnish

chili paste (optional)

1. In 6-quart saucepot, melt butter over medium heat. Add ginger, shallots, garlic, onion, and lemongrass, and cook until golden, about 8 minutes, stirring occasionally. Add broth, corn, sugar, salt, and water; heat to boiling over high heat. Reduce heat to low; cover and simmer 5 minutes. Discard lemongrass peel. Remove 2 cups soup; reserve.

2. In blender at low speed, with center part of cover removed to allow steam to escape, blend soup remaining in saucepot in small batches until very smooth. Pour soup into large bowl after each batch.

3. Return blended soup and reserved soup to same saucepot; stir in half-and-half. Heat over medium heat until hot, stirring occasionally. Serve with cilantro and chili paste, if you like.

**EACH SERVING:** About 110 calories, 4g protein, 16g carbohydrate, 4g total fat (1g saturated), 2g fiber, 4mg cholesterol, 410mg sodium

# Winter Vegetable Chowder

*We developed this recipe with the freezer in mind. You'll be making a double batch and freezing the extra for a weekday meal, ready whenever you are!*

**ACTIVE TIME:** 40 minutes
**TOTAL TIME:** 1 hour 15 minutes

**MAKES:** 8 main-dish servings

6 medium leeks

2 tablespoons olive oil

4 medium stalks celery, chopped

3 medium parsnips, peeled and chopped

2 medium red potatoes, cut into ½-inch pieces

2 pounds butternut squash, peeled, seeded, and cut into ½-inch pieces

2 cans (14½ ounces each) vegetable broth

4 cups water

½ teaspoon chopped fresh thyme

1 teaspoon salt

¾ teaspoon coarsely ground black pepper

1 cup half-and-half or light cream

thyme sprigs for garnish

## IT'S SO GOOD!

Like cucumbers, you don't normally think of celery having any other benefit but adding crunch. To the contrary, one cup raw celery is an excellent source of vitamin C and bone-protective vitamin K; it also contains iron, calcium, potassium, vitamin A, and many other nutrients.

1. Cut off roots and trim dark-green tops from leeks. Discard any tough outer leaves. Cut each leek lengthwise in half, then crosswise into ½-inch-thick slices. Rinse leeks in large bowl of cold water; swish to remove sand. With hands, transfer leeks to colander, leaving sand in bottom of bowl. Repeat rinsing and draining several times, until all sand is removed. Drain well.

2. In 6-quart saucepot, heat oil over medium-high heat until hot. Add leeks, celery, and parsnips, and cook until all vegetables are tender, 10 to 12 minutes stirring occasionally.

3. Add potatoes, squash, broth, water, chopped thyme, salt, and pepper; heat to boiling over medium-high heat. Reduce heat to medium-low; cover and simmer until potatoes and squash are tender, about 10 minutes.

4. Stir in half-and-half and heat through, about 13 minutes. Spoon half of soup into tureen and garnish with thyme sprigs.

5. Spoon remaining soup into freezer-safe containers and freeze. To reheat, thaw overnight in refrigerator or in microwave. To heat on stovetop, pour into saucepan, cover, and heat to boiling over medium, about 25 minutes, stirring often. To heat in microwave, pour into microwave-safe bowl, cover, and heat on Low (30 percent) 10 minutes, stirring once or twice, then on High 15 to 20 minutes, stirring once.

**EACH SERVING:** About 215 calories, 5g protein, 35g carbohydrate, 8g total fat (3g saturated), 5g fiber, 11mg cholesterol, 560mg sodium

# New Orleans Green Gumbo

*Popular around the Mississippi Delta, this soup has a slightly thickened "gumbo" texture created by the red pepper–spiked brown roux and grated potato.*

**ACTIVE TIME:** 40 minutes | **TOTAL TIME:** 1 hour

**MAKES:** 10 cups or 4 main-dish servings

2 tablespoons canola or light olive oil

¼ cup all-purpose flour

1 (32 ounce) container vegetable broth

1½ pounds fresh greens (collard and/or mustard), cleaned and cut into ½-inch pieces (see Cook's Tip, right)

2 teaspoons salt-free Cajun seasoning

1 teaspoon salt

1 package (10 ounces) frozen chopped spinach, thawed

1 large all-purpose potato (8 ounces), peeled and shredded

4 cups water

1 tablespoon cider vinegar

Hot sauce for serving

1. In 5-quart Dutch oven, heat oil over medium heat. Stir in flour and cook, stirring frequently, until golden brown, about 4 minutes. Remove from heat and gradually whisk in broth until blended.

2. Stir in greens, seasoning, salt, spinach, potato, and water; heat to boiling over high heat. Reduce heat to low; cover and simmer until soup thickens slightly and greens are tender, about 30 minutes.

3. Stir in vinegar and remove from heat. Ladle into bowls and serve with hot sauce.

**EACH SERVING:** About 214 calories, 7g protein, 30g carbohydrate, 8g total fat (0.5g saturated), 7g fiber, 0mg cholesterol, 1,624mg sodium

## COOK'S TIP

To streamline your soup-making time, wash, dry, and cut greens a day ahead; store them loosely wrapped in refrigerator.

# Country Vegetable Stew with Couscous Ⓥ

*Talk about eating a rainbow of vegetables! Chock-full of tomatoes, mushrooms, eggplant, carrots, and zucchini, this stew dishes up the full antioxidant spectrum, with a healthy dose of protein provided by the garbanzo beans.*

**ACTIVE TIME:** 25 minutes
**TOTAL TIME:** 1 hour 15 minutes
**MAKES:** 6 main-dish servings

1 pound white mushrooms
1 small eggplant (1 to 1¼ pounds)
1 bag (16 ounces) carrots, peeled
2 small zucchini (6 ounces each)
1 medium onion, peeled
6 teaspoons light corn-oil spread
1 can (28 ounces) plum tomatoes
1 teaspoon sugar
¾ teaspoon salt
½ teaspoon ground cumin
1 can (14½ ounces) vegetable broth
1 cup couscous (Moroccan pasta)
2 teaspoons chopped fresh parsley
1 tablespoon all-purpose flour
2 tablespoons water
1 can (15 to 19 ounces) garbanzo beans, rinsed and drained

1. Cut each mushroom in half. Cut eggplant into 1-inch chunks. Cut carrots into ¼-inch-thick slices. Cut zucchini into 1½-inch chunks. Coarsely chop onion.

2. In 5-quart Dutch oven or saucepot, heat 2 teaspoons corn-oil spread over medium-high heat. Add mushrooms and cook until golden brown and all liquid from mushrooms evaporates; remove to bowl. Heat 2 more teaspoons corn-oil spread in same Dutch oven, add eggplant and zucchini, and cook until golden brown; remove to bowl with mushrooms. Heat remaining 2 teaspoons corn-oil spread, add carrots and onion, and cook until golden brown. Stir in tomatoes with their juice, sugar, salt, and cumin, breaking tomatoes up with side of spoon; heat to boiling over high heat. Reduce heat to low; cover and simmer 10 minutes.

3. Add mushrooms, eggplant, zucchini, and any juices in bowl to Dutch oven; heat to boiling over high heat. Reduce heat to low; cover and simmer until vegetables are tender, about 10 minutes.

4. Meanwhile, in 2-quart saucepan, heat broth to boiling over high heat. Add couscous; cover and remove from heat. Let stand 5 minutes. Stir in parsley.

5. In cup, with fork, mix flour and water into smooth paste. Stir flour mixture and garbanzo beans into vegetables; heat to boiling over high heat. Boil until stew thickens slightly and beans are heated through, about 2 minutes. Serve stew over couscous.

**EACH SERVING:** About 360 calories, 14g protein, 70g carbohydrate, 4g total fat (0.5g saturated), 12g fiber, 0mg cholesterol, 1,088mg sodium

# Moroccan Vegetable Stew (V)

*A substantial stew starring skillet-browned carrots, squash, and onion — sweetened with cinnamon and prunes. This is delicious served over hot fluffy couscous.*

**ACTIVE TIME:** 25 minutes | **TOTAL TIME:** 35 minutes

**MAKES:** 4 main-dish servings

- 1 tablespoon olive oil
- 2 medium carrots, peeled and cut into ¼-inch-thick slices
- 1 medium butternut squash (1¾ pounds), peeled, seeded, and cut into 1-inch cubes
- 1 medium onion, chopped
- 1 can (15 to 19 ounces) garbanzo beans, rinsed and drained
- 1 can (14½ ounces) stewed tomatoes
- ½ cup pitted prunes, chopped
- ½ teaspoon ground cinnamon
- ½ teaspoon salt
- ⅛ teaspoon crushed red pepper, more to taste
- 1½ cups water
- 1 cup couscous (Moroccan pasta)
- 1 cup vegetable broth
- 2 tablespoons chopped fresh cilantro or parsley

1. In nonstick 12-inch skillet, heat oil over medium heat until hot. Add carrots, squash, and onion, and cook until golden, about 10 minutes, stirring frequently. Stir in garbanzo beans, stewed tomatoes with their juice, prunes, cinnamon, salt, crushed red pepper, and water; heat to boiling over high heat. Reduce heat to low; cover and simmer until vegetables are tender, about 30 minutes.

2. Meanwhile, prepare couscous as label directs but use vegetable broth in place of the water called for on label.

3. Stir cilantro into stew. Spoon stew over couscous to serve.

**EACH SERVING:** About 485 calories, 16g protein, 94g carbohydrate, 7g total fat (1g saturated), 15g fiber, 3mg cholesterol, 1,030mg sodium

# Moroccan Sweet Potato Stew Ⓥ

*With just two teaspoons of olive oil, this fragrant stew is heart-healthy and satisfying.*

**ACTIVE TIME:** 15 minutes | **TOTAL TIME:** 45 minutes
**MAKES:** 4 main-dish servings

2 teaspoons olive oil
1 medium yellow onion, chopped
3 garlic cloves, crushed with garlic press
1½ teaspoons curry powder
1½ teaspoons ground cumin
¼ teaspoon ground allspice

1 can (14½ ounces) diced tomatoes
1 can (14½ ounces reduced-sodium vegetable broth
1 cup no-salt-added garbanzo beans, rinsed and drained
1 large sweet potato (1 pound), peeled and cut into ¾-inch chunks
2 small zucchini (6 ounces each), cut into ¾-inch chunks
1 cup whole-grain couscous (Moroccan pasta)
¼ cup loosely packed fresh mint leaves, chopped

1. In nonstick 12-inch skillet, heat oil over medium heat until hot. Add onion and cook until tender and lightly browned, 8 to 10 minutes, stirring occasionally. Stir in garlic, curry powder, cumin, and allspice; cook 30 seconds.

2. Add tomatoes, broth, beans, and sweet potato; cover and heat to boiling over medium-high heat. Reduce heat to medium and cook 10 minutes.

3. Stir in zucchini, cover, and cook until vegetables are tender, about 10 minutes.

4. Meanwhile, prepare couscous as label directs.

5. Stir mint into stew. Serve stew with couscous.

**EACH SERVING:** About 360 calories, 14g protein, 70g carbohydrate, 5g total fat (1g saturated), 13g fiber, 0mg cholesterol, 670mg sodium

# Skillet Eggplant Stew

*If you like eggplant, you're going to love this—it's a thick, glazed, sweet-and-sour stew studded with olives and melted bits of mozzarella.*

**ACTIVE TIME:** 10 minutes | **TOTAL TIME:** 30 minutes

**MAKES:** 4 main-dish servings

3 tablespoons olive oil

1 large onion (12 ounces), cut into ¾-inch pieces

2 medium eggplants (1½ to 2 pounds each), cut into 2-inch pieces

½ cup pimiento-stuffed olives

2 tablespoons dark brown sugar

1 tablespoon balsamic vinegar

¾ teaspoon salt

½ cup water

1 package (9 ounces) fresh mozzarella cheese balls, drained and each cut in half

1 large ripe tomato (10 to 12 ounces), cut into ¾-inch pieces

¼ cup loosely packed fresh basil leaves, coarsely chopped

1. In nonstick 12-inch skillet (2 inches deep) or nonstick 5-quart saucepot, heat 1 tablespoon oil over medium heat until hot. Add onion and cook until golden, about 10 minutes, stirring occasionally.

2. Increase heat to medium-high. Add remaining 2 tablespoons oil and heat until hot. Add eggplant and cook until it is browned, about 10 minutes longer. Stir in olives, brown sugar, vinegar, salt, and water; heat to boiling. Reduce heat to low; cover and simmer until eggplant is tender, 10 to 15 minutes longer.

3. Remove skillet from heat; stir in mozzarella, tomato, and basil.

**EACH SERVING:** About 410 calories, 15g protein, 30g carbohydrate, 27g total fat (11g saturated), 15g fiber, 49mg cholesterol, 1,165mg sodium

---

## DOES RINSING CANNED BEANS REDUCE SODIUM?

Canned beans can't be beat when it comes to saving time and money. But if you're tracking your sodium, a can full of beans may be off-limits, packing more than 450 milligrams of sodium per half-cup.

Many people think that rinsing beans will significantly cut their saltiness. Are they full of beans? We wanted proof, so the Good Housekeeping Institute's Chemistry Department drained and rinsed 3 varieties by Goya and Progresso—red kidney, white kidney, and black—and then analyzed the amount of sodium remaining.

THE SURPRISE: Sodium was reduced in comparison to label claims, but results varied, with reductions generally between 16 and 30%. (For example, Progresso red kidney beans started out with 340mg sodium per serving and had 271mg after draining and rinsing.)

So if you want to rinse beans for a fresher taste (as we do in our test kitchens), keep it up. But don't count on this as a major salt-reducing step. If you're on a strict low-sodium diet, switch to dried beans—cooked without salt—or buy low-salt canned beans.

# Vegetable-Bean Stew Ⓥ

*Serve this with whole-grain couscous or brown rice to soak up all the flavorful liquid.*

**ACTIVE TIME:** 15 minutes | **TOTAL TIME:** 55 minutes
**MAKES:** 4 main-dish servings

1 tablespoon olive oil

1 medium onion, chopped

2 garlic cloves, crushed with garlic press

1½ teaspoons curry powder

1½ teaspoons ground cumin

¼ teaspoon salt

1 can (14½ ounces) diced tomatoes

1 can (14½ ounces) reduced-sodium vegetable broth

1 can (15 to 19 ounces) garbanzo beans, rinsed and drained

12 ounces carrots (3 medium), peeled and cut into 1-inch chunks

12 ounces parsnips (3 medium), peeled and cut into 1-inch chunks

1 cup water

1 large zucchini, cut into ½-inch chunks

¼ cup loosely packed fresh mint leaves, chopped

1. In 5- to 6-quart saucepot, heat oil over medium heat until hot. Add onion and cook until tender, 8 to 10 minutes, stirring occasionally. Stir in garlic, curry powder, cumin, and salt; cook 30 seconds, stirring. Add tomatoes with their juice, broth, garbanzo beans, carrots, parsnips, and water; heat to boiling over medium-high heat. Reduce heat to medium; cover and cook 10 minutes.

2. Stir in zucchini; cover and cook until vegetables are tender, 10 to 15 minutes longer.

3. Remove saucepot from heat; stir in mint.

**EACH SERVING:** About 335 calories, 12g protein, 62g carbohydrate, 6g total fat (1g saturated), 15g fiber, 0mg cholesterol, 1,030mg sodium

## IT'S SO GOOD!

When we think about the nutritional value of different ingredients, it's easy to overlook the onion. One cup of chopped onion is high in the mineral chromium, which is important to the regulation of your body's blood-sugar levels. It's also a good source of vitamin C and dietary fiber.

# Jalapeño-Spiked Black-Bean Soup Ⓥ

*This flavorful Tex-Mex soup uses the hand blender to make quick work of turning a chunky vegetable mixture into a delicious soup. Serve with a mixed green salad and warm flour tortillas for a perfect weeknight dinner. This soup is vegan if you skip the optional sour cream.*

**ACTIVE TIME:** 24 minutes | **TOTAL TIME:** 45 minutes

**MAKES:** 4 main-dish servings

- 1 tablespoon olive oil
- 1 medium onion, coarsely chopped
- 1 medium stalk celery, coarsely chopped
- 1 medium carrot, peeled and coarsely chopped
- 1 jalapeño chile, seeds and membranes discarded, coarsely chopped
- 2 garlic cloves, minced
- 1 teaspoon ground cumin
- 2 cans (15 to 19 ounces each) black beans, rinsed and drained
- 1 can (14½ ounces) vegetable broth
- 2 cups water
- ½ teaspoon salt
- 2 tablespoons fresh lime juice
- ½ cup loosely packed fresh cilantro leaves, chopped
- lime wedges and sour cream (optional)

1. In 4-quart saucepan, heat oil over medium heat until hot. Add onion, celery, carrot, and jalapeño, and cook until tender, about 10 minutes, stirring occasionally. Add garlic and cumin, and cook 1 minute, stirring. Stir in black beans, broth, water, and salt; heat to boiling over high heat. Reduce heat to low; simmer 15 minutes.

2. Remove saucepan from heat. Following manufacturer's directions, use hand blender to puree mixture in saucepan until almost smooth. Stir in lime juice and sprinkle with cilantro. Serve with lime wedges and sour cream, if you like.

**EACH SERVING:** About 220 calories, 12g protein, 43g carbohydrate, 5g total fat (1g saturated), 14g fiber, 0mg cholesterol, 1,400mg sodium

# Indian Lentil-Vegetable Stew ⓥ

*We love the warm flavor that garam masala brings to our lentil stew. This essential component of Indian and other South Asian cuisines is a sweet aromatic blend of dry-roasted ground spices that may include: coriander, green and black cardamom, cinnamon, cloves, bay leaves, nutmeg or mace, ginger, black pepper, and cumin. Our suggested substitution in the recipe works well, but it isn't quite as authentic.*

**ACTIVE TIME:** 25 minutes
**TOTAL TIME:** 1 hour 20 minutes

**MAKES:** 6 main-dish servings

1½ cups brown basmati rice

1 tablespoon vegetable oil

1 large onion (12 ounces), chopped

2 tablespoons minced, peeled fresh ginger

1½ teaspoons garam masala
  (or 1½ teaspoons curry powder plus
  ¼ teaspoon ground cinnamon)

1 garlic clove, chopped

4 cups water

2 cups green lentils, rinsed and picked over

1 pound sweet potatoes (1 large), peeled and
  cut into ½-inch chunks

1 can (14½ ounces) diced tomatoes

1 can (14½ ounces) vegetable broth

½ teaspoon salt

1 bag (9 ounces) fresh spinach, tough stems
  trimmed, or 1 package (10 ounces) frozen
  leaf spinach, thawed and squeezed dry

1. Prepare rice as label directs.

2. Meanwhile, in 6-quart saucepot, heat oil over medium heat until hot. Add onion and cook until tender and lightly browned, 8 to 10 minutes. Stir in ginger, garam masala, and garlic, and cook 1 minute. Add water, lentils, sweet potatoes, tomatoes with their juice, broth, and salt; heat to boiling over high heat. Reduce heat to low; cover and simmer until lentils and sweet potatoes are tender, about 25 minutes, stirring occasionally.

3. Add spinach to stew; heat through. Serve stew with rice.

**EACH SERVING:** About 520 calories, 25g protein, 97g carbohydrate, 5g total fat (0g saturated), 17g fiber, 0mg cholesterol, 675mg sodium

## IT'S SO GOOD!

Make sweet potatoes a regular part of your recipe rotation. One small cooked sweet potato is an excellent source of vitamin A, which contributes to a healthy immune system, as well as healthy bones and eyes. Sweet potatoes also contain vitamin C, bone-building manganese, dietary fiber, and potassium.

# Gingery Spinach-Lentil Stew Ⓥ

*If you're in the mood for lentils but don't have all the veggies for the previous recipe, try this one. It's still fragrant with the warming spices of India and serves up a deliciously healthy dose of greens as well. This stew is vegan if you skip the optional yogurt.*

**ACTIVE TIME:** 15 minutes | **TOTAL TIME:** 55 minutes
**MAKES:** 6 main-dish servings

- 1 tablespoon olive oil
- 4 garlic cloves, crushed with garlic press
- 1 large onion (12 ounces), chopped
- 2 tablespoons grated, peeled fresh ginger
- 2 teaspoons ground coriander
- 2 teaspoons ground cumin
- ¼ teaspoon turmeric
- 4 cups water
- 1 can (14½ ounces) diced tomatoes
- 1 can (14½ ounces) vegetable broth
- 1 package (16 ounces) lentils, rinsed and picked over
- 1 teaspoon salt
- 2 packages (10 ounces each) frozen chopped spinach, thawed and squeezed dry
- plain low-fat yogurt (optional)

**1.** In 4-quart saucepan, heat oil over medium heat until hot. Add garlic, onion, and ginger, and cook until tender and golden, 8 to 10 minutes, stirring frequently. Stir in coriander, cumin, and turmeric, and cook 30 seconds, stirring. Stir in water, tomatoes with their juice, broth, lentils, and salt; heat to boiling over high heat. Reduce heat to medium-low; simmer until lentils are tender, 25 to 30 minutes.

**2.** Stir in spinach. Heat over medium heat until hot.

**3.** Spoon stew into bowls. Serve with a dollop of yogurt, if you like.

**EACH SERVING:** About 340 calories, 26g protein, 53g carbohydrate, 4g total fat (0g saturated), 27g fiber, 0mg cholesterol, 1,085mg sodium

# Three-Bean Vegetable Chili Ⓥ

*This chili is so good, we doubled the recipe. You can find edamame beans in the freezer case of most large supermarkets. This recipe is vegan if you skip the optional sour cream and Cheddar.*

**ACTIVE TIME:** 35 minutes
**TOTAL TIME:** 1 hour 5 minutes

**MAKES:** 8 main-dish servings

1 tablespoon vegetable oil

1 pound carrots, peeled and cut into ½-inch dice

2 large stalks celery, sliced

2 garlic cloves, crushed with garlic press

1 jumbo onion (1 pound), chopped

4 teaspoons chili powder

1 tablespoon ground cumin

½ teaspoon ground cinnamon

¼ teaspoon ground red pepper (cayenne)

1 teaspoon salt

1 can (14½ ounces) diced tomatoes

1 can (14½ ounces) vegetable broth

1 cup water

2 cans (15 to 19 ounces) white kidney beans (cannellini), rinsed and drained

1 can (15 to 19 ounces) pink beans, rinsed and drained

2 cups frozen shelled edamame (soybeans)

¼ cup (plus additional leaves for garnish) fresh cilantro leaves, chopped

reduced-fat sour cream and shredded reduced-fat Cheddar cheese (optional)

1. In 5- to 6-quart Dutch oven, heat oil over medium-high heat until hot. Add carrots, celery, garlic, and onion, and cook until tender and browned, 10 to 12 minutes, stirring occasionally. Stir in chili powder, cumin, cinnamon, ground red pepper, and salt; cook 30 seconds, stirring. Add tomatoes and their juice, broth, and water; heat to boiling over high heat. Reduce heat to low; cover and simmer 15 minutes.

2. Stir kidney and pink beans into Dutch oven; cover and cook 10 minutes longer. Stir in edamame and cook, uncovered, until edamame are just tender, 5 to 7 minutes, stirring occasionally.

3. Stir chopped cilantro into chili. Spoon half of chili into serving bowls; garnish with cilantro leaves. Serve with sour cream and Cheddar, if you like.

4. Spoon remaining chili into freezer-safe containers and freeze. To reheat, thaw overnight in refrigerator or in microwave. To heat on stovetop, pour into saucepan, cover, and heat to boiling over medium heat, about 30 minutes, stirring occasionally. To heat in microwave, pour into microwave-safe bowl, cover, and heat on Low (30 percent) 10 minutes, stirring once or twice, then on High 5 to 10 minutes, stirring once.

**EACH SERVING:** About 345 calories, 19g protein, 51g carbohydrate, 8g total fat (1g saturated), 15g fiber, 0mg cholesterol, 945mg sodium

# Squash and Black Bean Chili Ⓥ

*A spicy blend of squash, carrots, black beans, and more — you'll never miss the meat! This recipe is vegan if you skip the optional sour cream.*

**ACTIVE TIME:** 35 minutes | **TOTAL TIME:** 50 minutes

**MAKES:** 6 main-dish servings

4 teaspoons olive oil

1 medium butternut squash (1¾ pounds), peeled, seeded, and cut into ¾-inch cubes (see Cook's Tip, right)

2 medium carrots, peeled and diced

1 medium onion, diced

3 tablespoons chili powder

1 can (28 ounces) plum tomatoes

1 can (4 ounces) chopped mild green chiles

1 cup vegetable broth

¼ teaspoon salt

2 cans (15 to 19 ounces each) black beans, rinsed and drained

¼ cup chopped fresh cilantro

4 tablespoons nonfat sour cream (optional)

**1.** In 5-quart Dutch oven, heat 2 teaspoons oil over medium-high heat until hot. Add squash and cook until golden, stirring occasionally; remove squash to bowl.

**2.** In same Dutch oven, heat remaining 2 teaspoons oil until hot; cook carrots and onion until well browned. Stir in chili powder; cook 1 minute, stirring. Add tomatoes with their juice, chiles with their liquid, broth, and salt; heat to boiling over high heat. Reduce heat to low; cover and simmer 30 minutes, stirring occasionally with spoon to break up tomatoes.

**3.** Stir in black beans and squash; heat to boiling over high heat. Reduce heat to low; cover and simmer until squash is tender and chili thickens, about 15 minutes. Stir in cilantro and serve with sour cream, if you like.

**EACH SERVING:** About 225 calories, 14g protein, 44g carbohydrate, 5g total fat (1g saturated), 15g fiber, 0mg cholesterol, 930mg sodium

## COOK'S TIP

To peel butternut squash, use a chef's knife to cut off the top and bottom ends of the squash. Then cut the squash in two, at the point where the narrow part (the neck) meets the rounded bottom. Cut the bottom in half and, with a spoon, scoop out the seeds from both halves. Using a sharp, swivel-blade Y-shaped vegetable peeler, remove the peel from the two bottom halves and the neck. No peeler? Place the bottom halves cut side down; cut into 1½- to 2-inch-wide slices, then cut away the tough skin from each slice with a paring knife. Repeat with the neck of the squash. Finally, dice, slice, or cut the squash flesh into chunks, as your recipe directs.

# White-Bean and Tomatillo Chili (V)

*This spicy chili is made with fresh tomatillos—the tart, green, tomatolike fruits (with papery husks) that are a staple of Southwestern cuisine. Serve with warm tortillas and a dollop of plain yogurt—nondairy yogurt makes it vegan.*

**ACTIVE TIME:** 25 minutes | **TOTAL TIME:** 45 minutes

**MAKES:** 4 main-dish servings

- 2 tablespoons olive oil
- 3 garlic cloves, crushed with garlic press
- 1 small onion, cut in half and thinly sliced
- 1 jalapeño chile, seeded and minced
- 1 teaspoon ground cumin
- 1 pound tomatillos, husked, rinsed, and coarsely chopped
- 1¼ teaspoons salt
- ½ teaspoon sugar
- 1 can (14½ ounces) vegetable broth
- 1 can (4 ounces) chopped mild green chiles
- 1 cup water
- 2 cans (15 to 19 ounces each) white kidney beans (cannellini), rinsed, drained, and coarsely mashed
- 1 cup loosely packed fresh cilantro leaves, chopped
- 4 warm tortillas (optional)
- 4 tablespoons plain yogurt (optional)

1. In nonstick 10-inch skillet, heat oil over medium heat until hot. Add garlic, onion, jalapeño, and cumin, and cook until light golden, 7 to 10 minutes, stirring often.

2. Meanwhile, in 5- to 6-quart saucepot, heat tomatillos, salt, sugar, broth, green chiles and their liquid broth, and water to boiling over high heat. Reduce heat to low. Stir onion mixture into saucepot; cover and simmer 15 minutes.

3. Stir in beans and cilantro; heat through. Serve with warm tortillas and a dollop of yogurt, if you like.

**EACH SERVING:** About 335 calories, 13g protein, 50g carbohydrate, 10g total fat (1g saturated), 15g fiber, 0mg cholesterol, 1,610mg sodium

# 5

# Stir-Fries & Sautés

These dishes are just right for weeknight cooking. All of them can be made, start to finish, in less than an hour and plenty of them come together in under 30 minutes. This is your go-to chapter when you're shuttling between one child's track meet and another's dance lesson.

Stir-fries are a tasty way to cook up all sorts of healthful and delicious vegetables. Feel free to substitute veggies you have on hand or add your favorites; snow peas, asparagus, cauliflower or broccoli flowerets, carrots, bell peppers—they're all wonderful thrown into a hot pan and cooked just until tender-crisp.

For added protein and iron, you can add cubed extra-firm tofu. Be sure to pat the tofu dry before adding it to the pan so that it browns nicely. And don't stir it too vigorously, or it'll start to come apart. A handful of toasted nuts—cashews or walnuts, peanuts or pistachios, depending on the dish—will also rev up the protein. Serve these stir-fries over white rice or experiment with whole grains, from brown rice or bulgur to farro or millet. Pasta, including whole-wheat couscous, makes an equally good base.

This chapter also serves up a selection of saucy sautés and stovetop braises, including meatless versions of comfort food classics like shepherd's pie and stuffed cabbage.

*Clockwise from top left: Warm Broccoli and Carrot Slaw (page 143); Vegetable Curry (page 133); Lo Mein with Tofu, Snow Peas, and Carrots (page 136); Potato Dumplings with Cabbage and Apples (page 138)*

# Japanese Eggplant and Tofu Stir-Fry ⓥ

*Japanese eggplant is long and slender, with tender flesh and bright purple skin. When cooked, the eggplant absorbs the wonderful flavor of the stir-fry sauce. Pair it with brown rice or bulgur to soak up all the juices.*

**ACTIVE TIME:** 30 minutes
**TOTAL TIME:** 45 minutes plus standing
**MAKES:** 4 main-dish servings

1 package (16 ounces) extra-firm tofu, drained and cut into 1-inch cubes

½ cup plus ⅓ cup water

1 cup vegetable broth

¼ cup reduced-sodium soy sauce

2 tablespoons brown sugar

2 tablespoons cornstarch

2 tablespoons vegetable oil

4 medium Japanese eggplants (4 ounces each), cut diagonally into 2-inch chunks

8 ounces shiitake mushrooms, stems removed and caps cut into quarters

1 tablespoon grated, peeled fresh ginger

3 garlic cloves, crushed with garlic press

3 green onions, thinly sliced

2 heads baby bok choy (6 ounces each), cut crosswise into 1-inch-thick slices

1. In medium bowl, place four layers paper towel; add tofu and cover with four more layers paper towel, pressing lightly to extract liquid from tofu. Let tofu stand 10 minutes to drain.

2. Meanwhile, in 2-cup liquid measuring cup, with fork or wire whisk, combine ½ cup water, broth, soy sauce, brown sugar, and cornstarch, stirring until brown sugar and cornstarch are dissolved; set aside.

3. In deep, 12-inch skillet or wok, heat 1 tablespoon oil over medium-high heat until hot. Add eggplant and remaining ⅓ cup water; cover and cook until eggplant is tender, 7 to 10 minutes, stirring occasionally. Transfer eggplant to small bowl; set aside.

4. Add remaining 1 tablespoon oil to skillet and heat until hot. Add mushrooms and tofu, and cook until tofu is lightly browned, about 5 minutes. Stir in ginger, garlic, and half of green onions; cook 1 minute, stirring. Add bok choy, and cook until vegetables are lightly browned, about 4 minutes longer, stirring occasionally.

5. Stir vegetable-broth mixture to blend; add to tofu mixture with eggplant. Heat to boiling over medium-high heat; reduce heat to low and simmer 1 minute, stirring. Sprinkle with remaining green onions before serving.

**EACH SERVING:** About 280 calories, 15g protein, 33g carbohydrate, 13g total fat (1g saturated), 5g fiber, 0mg cholesterol, 865mg sodium

# Tofu in Spicy Brown Sauce Ⓥ

*We used a package of frozen Asian-style vegetables to save chopping time. For best quality, buy firm tofu sold in sealed packages.*

**ACTIVE TIME:** 15 minutes | **TOTAL TIME:** 35 minutes
**MAKES:** 6 main-dish servings

- 2 packages (16 ounces each) extra-firm tofu, drained
- 1 cup vegetable broth
- 1/3 cup reduced-sodium soy sauce
- 1 tablespoon brown sugar
- 1 tablespoon cornstarch
- 2 tablespoons seasoned rice vinegar
- 1/8 teaspoon crushed red pepper
- 1/2 cup cold water
- 1 package (16 ounces) frozen Asian-style vegetables
- 1 tablespoon vegetable oil
- 3 garlic cloves, crushed with garlic press
- 2 tablespoons minced, peeled fresh ginger
- 3 green onions, sliced
- steamed white rice (optional)

## IT'S SO GOOD!

Ginger contains phytonutrients called gingerols. These compounds are known for their powerful anti-inflammatory properties.

1. Place four layers paper towel in 15½" by 10½" jelly-roll pan. Cut each piece of tofu horizontally in half. Place tofu on towels in pan; top with four more layers paper towel. Gently press tofu with hand to extract excess moisture. Let stand 1 minute; repeat once, using more paper towels. Cut tofu into ½-inch dice; set aside.

2. In 2-cup glass measuring cup, with fork or wire whisk, combine broth, soy sauce, brown sugar, cornstarch, vinegar, crushed red pepper, and water, stirring until sugar and cornstarch are dissolved.

3. In nonstick 12-inch skillet, heat frozen vegetables, covered, over medium heat 5 minutes, stirring occasionally. Uncover and cook until liquid evaporates, about 2 minutes longer, stirring occasionally. Transfer vegetables to bowl. Wipe skillet dry.

4. In same skillet, heat oil over medium heat until hot. Add garlic and ginger; cook 1 minute. Stir broth mixture; add to skillet and heat to boiling over medium-high heat, stirring. Boil 1 minute. Stir in vegetables and tofu, and cook until heated through, about 5 minutes. Sprinkle with green onions before serving. Serve with steamed rice, if you like.

**EACH SERVING WITHOUT RICE:** About 295 calories, 27g protein, 20g carbohydrate, 16g total fat (2g saturated), 4g fiber, 0mg cholesterol, 870mg sodium

# Thai Tofu Stir-Fry  ⓥ

*Stir-fry the tofu gently so it maintains its shape as it browns.*

**ACTIVE TIME:** 35 minutes | **TOTAL TIME:** 1 hour
**MAKES:** 4 main-dish servings

1 package (16 ounces) extra-firm tofu, drained, patted dry, and cut into 1-inch cubes

1 tablespoon curry powder

1 tablespoon grated, peeled fresh ginger

1 tablespoon soy sauce

1 tablespoon fresh lime juice

6 teaspoons vegetable oil

1 medium head bok choy (1 pound), sliced crosswise into 1-inch slices

1 medium zucchini (8 to 10 ounces), cut into bite-size pieces

3 green onions, cut into 2-inch pieces

1 package (8 ounces) medium mushrooms, cut into ¼-inch-thick slices

1 medium red pepper (4 to 6 ounces), sliced

¾ cup vegetable broth

1½ teaspoons cornstarch

½ cup packed fresh basil leaves, chopped

1. In medium bowl, gently toss tofu cubes with curry powder, ginger, soy sauce, and lime juice.

2. In 12-inch skillet, heat 2 teaspoons oil over medium-high heat until hot. Add bok choy, zucchini, and green onions, and cook until vegetables are tender-crisp, about 8 minutes. Remove vegetables to large bowl.

3. With slotted spoon, remove tofu from curry mixture; reserve curry mixture. In same skillet, heat 2 more teaspoons oil. Add tofu and cook until lightly browned, about 5 minutes, gently stirring a few times. Remove tofu to bowl with bok-choy mixture.

4. In same skillet, heat remaining 2 teaspoons oil. Add mushrooms and red pepper, and cook until pepper is tender-crisp, about 8 minutes.

5. Into curry mixture in bowl, stir broth and cornstarch until cornstarch is dissolved. Stir into skillet with mushroom mixture and heat to boiling; boil 1 minute, until sauce thickens slightly. Return bok-choy mixture to skillet. Add basil; heat through before serving.

**EACH SERVING:** About 295 calories, 15g protein, 17g carbohydrate, 18g total fat (2g saturated), 6g fiber, 2mg cholesterol, 745mg sodium

# Stir-Fried Broccoli with Pasta

*This is a wonderful way to get your kids to eat their broccoli. It's cooked just until tender-crisp, then served with pasta and a sprinkling of Parmesan and toasted pine nuts.*

**ACTIVE TIME:** 30 minutes | **TOTAL TIME:** 45 minutes
**MAKES:** 4 main-dish servings

12 ounces cavatelli or ziti

3 teaspoons salt

2 medium bunches broccoli (1 pound each)

3 tablespoons olive oil

2 garlic cloves, minced

½ teaspoon crushed red pepper

⅓ cup water

½ cup freshly grated Parmesan cheese

1 jar (3 ounces) pine nuts (pignoli), toasted, or ½ cup chopped toasted walnuts

# KNOW YOUR SOY

You can find these heart-healthy products in health-food stores, specialty markets, and large supermarkets:

✦ **TOFU:** This is soybean curd that is drained and pressed in a process similar to cheese-making. The creamiest tofu (with the least liquid pressed out) is *soft* or *silken*. Use it in shakes, dressings, and dips. Extracting still more liquid produces regular tofu, then *firm*, and finally *extra-firm* tofu, which are all excellent grilled or in stir-fries. Look for nonfat, low-fat, and full-fat varieties. Avoid bulk tofu, unpackaged blocks sold in water; it can be contaminated with bacteria. Sealed water-packed tofu and the aseptically packaged kind (unrefrigerated) are much safer. To store tofu after opening, cover with cool water and refrigerate for up to 1 week; change the water daily.

✦ **TEMPEH (TEHM-pay):** A dense, chewy cake, this meat alternative is made from cooked, fermented soybeans. Like other soy products, tempeh absorbs the flavor of the ingredients it's cooked with, even though it has a smoky flavor of its own. Tempeh is sold refrigerated or frozen; try it in soups or stir-fries.

✦ **TEXTURED VEGETABLE PROTEIN (TVP):** Also known as textured soy protein, these dried granules made from defatted soy flakes have to be rehydrated in water before cooking (see Hearty Pasta and Vegetables, page 212). Commercially, TVP is used to make soy hot dogs and veggie burgers.

1. Heat medium covered saucepot of *water* plus 2 teaspoons salt to boiling over high heat. Add cavatelli and cook as label directs. Drain pasta, reserving *1 cup cooking water*. Return cavatelli to saucepot; set aside.

2. Meanwhile, cut broccoli into 2½" by 1" pieces. In 12-inch skillet, heat oil over high heat until hot. Cook broccoli, stirring quickly and constantly, until evenly coated with oil. Add garlic, crushed red pepper, remaining 1 teaspoon salt, and ⅓ cup water. Reduce heat to medium; cover and cook 2 minutes. Uncover and cook, stirring, until broccoli is tender-crisp, about 5 minutes.

3. Over medium-high heat, toss broccoli mixture and reserved pasta cooking water with cavatelli to heat through. Remove saucepot from heat; stir in Parmesan. Sprinkle with toasted pine nuts.

**EACH SERVING:** About 690 calories, 27g protein, 87g carbohydrate, 30g total fat (5g saturated), 11g fiber, 9mg cholesterol, 985mg sodium

Ⓥ MAKE IT VEGAN: *Omit the Parmesan.*

# Vegetable Curry

*Korma is a mild, creamy yogurt-based sauce; jalfrezi is tomato-based. You can find Indian simmer sauces in specialty food stores as well as in the Asian foods section of many larger supermarkets. To create a surprising, colorful mix — the easy way — use packages of fresh precut produce.*

**ACTIVE TIME:** 10 minutes | **TOTAL TIME:** 15 minutes
**MAKES:** 4 main-dish servings

- 1 package (16 ounces) mixed fresh vegetables for stir-fry
- 1 bunch green onions, cut into 2-inch pieces
- ½ cup cold water
- 1 can (15 to 19 ounces) garbanzo beans, rinsed and drained
- 1 jar (15 ounces) Indian korma sauce or jalfrezi red pepper sauce, or one 10-ounce can plus ½ cup water
- 1 cup loosely packed fresh cilantro leaves

1. In 12-inch skillet, combine mixed vegetables and green onions; stir in water. Cover skillet and cook over medium-high heat until vegetables are tender-crisp, about 5 minutes, stirring occasionally.

2. Stir garbanzo beans and korma sauce into vegetable mixture in skillet. Cover and heat to boiling, stirring occasionally.

3. Remove skillet from heat; stir in cilantro leaves to serve.

**EACH SERVING:** About 360 calories, 12g protein, 57g carbohydrate, 10g total fat (5g saturated), 12g fiber, 2mg cholesterol, 730mg sodium

# Vegetarian Stuffed Cabbage Ⓥ

*You'll never miss the meat in this recipe. These cabbage leaves are stuffed with a savory mix of bell peppers, white beans, water chestnuts, and fresh ginger.*

**ACTIVE TIME:** 1 hour 10 minutes
**TOTAL TIME:** 1 hour 30 minutes
**MAKES:** 4 main-dish servings

1 large head savoy cabbage (3½ to 4 pounds)

1 tablespoon vegetable oil

1 medium red pepper (4 to 6 ounces), finely chopped

1 medium yellow pepper (4 to 6 ounces), finely chopped

1 medium onion, finely chopped

1 tablespoon seasoned rice vinegar

1 teaspoon reduced-sodium soy sauce

2 teaspoons minced, peeled fresh ginger

1 can (15 to 19 ounces) white kidney beans (cannellini), rinsed and drained

1 can (8 ounces) sliced water chestnuts, drained and finely chopped

2 cans (14½ ounces) stewed tomatoes

1 teaspoon sugar

1. Discard tough outer leaves from cabbage; with sharp knife, remove core. Fill 8-quart saucepot three-fourths full with *water*; heat to boiling over high heat. Place cabbage in *water*, cut-side up. Using two large spoons or forks, gently separate leaves as outer leaves soften slightly. When about three-fourths of the leaves have separated from cabbage, remove remaining head of cabbage from saucepot and set aside. Boil separated cabbage leaves, covered, until very tender, 10 to 12 minutes. Drain leaves in colander.

2. With knife, trim tough center rib from each cabbage leaf. Reserve 8 large leaves for rolls (if leaves are not very large, you may need to reserve 2 leaves for each roll). Coarsely slice enough of remaining cabbage leaves to make 2 cups for filling, reserving rest of cabbage for use another day.

3. In 12-inch skillet, heat oil over medium-high heat until hot. Add red and yellow peppers and onion, and cook until tender and lightly browned, 8 to 10 minutes. Add sliced cabbage, vinegar, soy sauce, and ginger; cook 5 minutes. Stir in kidney beans and water chestnuts. Let cabbage filling cool slightly.

4. On center of each reserved cabbage leaf, place a scant ½ cup filling. Fold two sides of cabbage leaf over filling, overlapping edges; roll jelly-roll fashion.

5. In same skillet, heat tomatoes with their juice and sugar to boiling over high heat, breaking up tomatoes with side of spoon. Add cabbage rolls. Reduce heat to low; cover and simmer until cabbage rolls are heated through, 10 to 15 minutes.

**EACH SERVING:** About 260 calories, 9g protein, 47g carbohydrate, 5g total fat (0.5g saturated), 12g fiber, 0mg cholesterol, 845mg sodium

# Unstuffed Cabbage ⓥ

*Cabbage wedges are microwaved, then topped with a sweet-and-sour tomato sauce—a simplified version of the classic stuffed cabbage. This is delicious served over brown rice or an aromatic rice blend.*

**ACTIVE TIME:** 20 minutes | **TOTAL TIME:** 40 minutes

**MAKES:** 4 main-dish servings

- 1 small head savoy cabbage (1½ pounds), tough outer leaves discarded, cored, and cut into 4 wedges
- ¼ cup water
- 1 tablespoon olive oil
- 2 medium carrots, peeled and chopped
- 2 medium stalks celery, chopped
- 1 medium red pepper (4 to 6 ounces), chopped
- 3 garlic cloves, crushed with garlic press
- 3 green onions, thinly sliced
- 1 tablespoon minced, peeled fresh ginger
- 1 can (14½ ounces) diced tomatoes
- 2 tablespoons soy sauce
- 2 tablespoons seasoned rice vinegar
- 1 tablespoon light brown sugar

1. Place cabbage in 3-quart microwave-safe baking dish; cover and cook in microwave oven on High 12 to 14 minutes, until cabbage is fork-tender.

2. Meanwhile, in 12-inch skillet, heat oil over medium-high heat until hot. Add carrots, celery, and red pepper; cook until vegetables are tender and golden, about 12 minutes. Add garlic, green onions, and ginger; cook 2 minutes, stirring. Add tomatoes with their juice, soy sauce, vinegar, and brown sugar; heat to boiling over medium-high heat. Reduce heat to medium-low and simmer 5 minutes, stirring occasionally.

3. Spoon tomato mixture over cabbage in baking dish; cover and cook in microwave on High 2 minutes to blend flavors.

**EACH SERVING:** About 145 calories, 6g protein, 26g carbohydrate, 4g total fat (1g saturated), 7g fiber, 0mg cholesterol, 1,200mg sodium

2 packages (3 ounces each) Oriental-flavor ramen noodles

2 teaspoons vegetable oil

1 package (16 ounces) extra-firm tofu, drained, patted dry, and diced

6 ounces (2 cups) snow peas, strings removed and each cut diagonally in half

3 green onions, cut into 2-inch pieces

1 package (5 ounces) shredded carrots (1½ cups)

½ cup bottled stir-fry sauce

3 ounces fresh bean sprouts (1 cup), rinsed and drained

1. Heat 4-quart covered saucepot of *water* to boiling over high heat. Add ramen noodles (reserve flavor packets) and cook 2 minutes. Drain noodles, reserving *¼ cup cooking water*.

2. Meanwhile, in 12-inch skillet, heat oil over medium-high heat until very hot. Add tofu and cook until lightly browned, 5 to 6 minutes, gently stirring a few times. Add snow peas and green onions; cook until vegetables are tender-crisp, 3 to 5 minutes, stirring frequently. Stir in carrots, stir-fry sauce, and contents of 1 ramen flavor packet to taste (depending on salt level of sauce), and cook until carrots are tender, about 2 minutes. (Discard remaining flavor packet or save for another use.)

3. Reserve some bean sprouts for garnish. Add noodles, reserved noodle cooking water, and remaining bean sprouts to skillet; cook 1 minute to blend flavors, stirring. Sprinkle with reserved bean sprouts to serve.

**EACH SERVING:** About 375 calories, 18g protein, 47g carbohydrate, 12g total fat (3g saturated), 4g fiber, 0mg cholesterol, 1,485mg sodium

# Lo Mein with Tofu, Snow Peas, and Carrots Ⓥ

*Packaged ramen noodles can be a great short-cut ingredient. Here they're combined with tofu, snow peas, carrots, and bean sprouts for a tasty homemade lo mein.*

**TOTAL TIME:** 15 minutes

**MAKES:** 4 main-dish servings

# Vegetable Lo Mein Ⓥ

*Try serving this with sliced oranges; they make a refreshing accompaniment.*

**TOTAL TIME:** 20 minutes

**MAKES:** 4 main-dish servings

- 1 package (16 ounces) linguine or spaghetti
- ⅓ cup hoisin sauce
- 2 tablespoons reduced-sodium soy sauce
- ½ teaspoon cornstarch
- 3 teaspoons vegetable oil
- 1 package (10 ounces) sliced mushrooms
- 1 tablespoon peeled, grated fresh ginger
- 1 package (10 ounces) shredded carrots
- 3 small zucchini (6 ounces each), each cut lengthwise in half, then cut crosswise into ¼-inch-thick slices
- 3 green onions, cut into 1-inch pieces
- 1 cup reduced-sodium vegetable broth
- 2 tablespoons seasoned rice vinegar

1. Prepare linguine as label directs but do not add salt to water.

2. Meanwhile, in cup, with fork or wire whisk, combine hoisin sauce, soy sauce, and cornstarch, stirring until cornstarch is dissolved, set aside.

3. In 12-inch skillet, heat 2 teaspoons oil over medium-high heat until hot. Add mushrooms and cook until they are golden and their liquid evaporates, about 5 minutes, stirring frequently. Stir in ginger; cook 30 seconds. Remove mushroom mixture to bowl.

4. In same skillet, heat remaining 1 teaspoon oil until hot. Add carrots and cook 2 minutes, stirring frequently. Stir in zucchini and green onions, and cook until vegetables are tender-crisp, about 10 minutes longer. Stir in broth, cornstarch mixture, and mushroom mixture. Heat to boiling; boil 1 minute, until sauce thickens.

5. To serve, toss linguine, vegetable mixture, and vinegar together in large serving bowl.

**EACH SERVING:** About 570 calories, 20g protein, 111g carbohydrate, 7g total fat (1g saturated), 1g fiber, 1mg cholesterol, 970mg sodium

# Potato Dumplings with Cabbage and Apples

Pierogi, *Polish-style comfort food, are usually filled with meat, seafood, cheese, potatoes, or mushrooms. They can be quite time-consuming to prepare from scratch, but fortunately, excellent frozen varieties are available.*

**ACTIVE TIME:** 12 minutes | **TOTAL TIME:** 25 minutes
**MAKES:** 4 main-dish servings

1 package (16 to 19 ounces) frozen potato-and-onion pierogi
1 tablespoon butter or margarine
1 small onion, thinly sliced
1 small head green cabbage (1½ pounds), trimmed, cored, and sliced
½ cup vegetable broth
½ teaspoon salt
2 medium MacIntosh apples (about 12 ounces)
2 teaspoons cider vinegar
1 tablespoon chopped fresh dill

1. In large saucepot, cook pierogi as label directs.

2. Meanwhile, in nonstick 12-inch skillet, melt butter over medium-low heat. Add onion and cook, stirring occasionally, until onion is tender and lightly browned, about 7 minutes.

3. Increase heat to medium; add cabbage, broth, and salt, and cook until cabbage is tender, about 10 minutes. While cabbage is cooking, core and cut apples into ¼-inch-thick wedges.

4. Add apples and vinegar to skillet with cabbage, and cook until apples soften, about 5 minutes.

5. Drain pierogi; toss with cabbage mixture and dill.

**EACH SERVING:** About 355 calories, 9g protein, 64g carbohydrate, 7g total fat (3g saturated), 2g fiber, 8mg cholesterol, 941mg sodium

# Vegetarian Bean Burritos

*Why go out for burritos when you can make them yourself in minutes?*

**ACTIVE TIME:** 10 minutes | **TOTAL TIME:** 20 minutes

**MAKES:** 4 main-dish servings

- 4 (10-inch) flour tortillas
- 2 teaspoons vegetable oil
- 4 medium zucchini (8 to 10 ounces each), each cut lengthwise in half, then sliced crosswise
- ¼ teaspoon salt
- ¼ teaspoon ground cinnamon
- 1 can (15 ounces) Spanish-style red kidney beans
- 1 can (15 to 19 ounces) black beans, rinsed and drained
- 4 ounces Monterey Jack cheese, shredded (1 cup)
- ½ cup loosely packed fresh cilantro leaves
- 1 jar (16 ounces) chunky-style salsa

1. Warm tortillas as label directs; keep warm.

2. In 12-inch skillet, heat oil over medium-high heat until hot. Add zucchini, salt, and cinnamon and cook until zucchini is tender-crisp, about 5 minutes.

3. Meanwhile, in 2-quart saucepan, heat kidney beans with their sauce and black beans just to simmering over medium heat; keep warm.

4. To serve, allow each person to assemble burrito as desired, using a warm tortilla, zucchini, bean mixture, Monterey Jack, and cilantro. Pass salsa to serve with burritos.

**EACH SERVING:** About 550 calories, 29g protein, 77g carbohydrate, 17g total fat (1g saturated), 19g fiber, 25mg cholesterol, 1,943mg sodium

Ⓥ **MAKE IT VEGAN:** *Omit the Monterey Jack.*

## IT'S SO GOOD!

The legumes, to a great degree, share approximately the same nutritional profile, though there are some differences. Red kidney beans and black beans are both high in folic acid, sleep-inducing tryptophan, bone-building manganese, protein, and dietary fiber. Red beans, however, offer almost 9% more of the daily recommended value of iron (28.9% versus 20.1%).

# Acorn Squash with White Beans and Sage ⓥ

*Preparation of this dish is easy and fast because the beans cook on the stovetop while the squash steams in the microwave. Round out the meal with some sautéed garlicky greens or salad tossed with lemony vinaigrette. This recipe is vegan if you skip the optional Parmesan.*

**ACTIVE TIME:** 30 minutes | **TOTAL TIME:** 35 minutes
**MAKES:** 4 main-dish servings

1 tablespoon olive oil

1 jumbo onion (1 pound), cut into ¼-inch dice

1 medium carrot, cut into ¼-inch dice

2 garlic cloves, crushed with garlic press

1 can (15 to 19 ounces) white kidney beans (cannellini), rinsed and drained

¾ cup vegetable broth

¼ teaspoon salt

¼ teaspoon coarsely ground black pepper

3 teaspoons chopped fresh sage

2 small acorn squashes (12 ounces each)

1 ripe medium tomato (6 to 8 ounces), cut into ¼-inch dice

sage sprigs for garnish

freshly grated Parmesan cheese (optional)

1. In 12-inch skillet, heat oil over medium-high heat until hot. Add onion, carrot, and garlic, and cook until vegetables are tender and golden, about 15 minutes, stirring occasionally. Add kidney beans, broth, salt, pepper, and 2 teaspoons chopped sage; heat to boiling. Cover skillet and keep warm.

2. Meanwhile, cut each squash lengthwise in half and remove seeds and strings. Place squash halves, cut side down, in 3-quart microwave-safe baking dish. Cover and cook in microwave oven on High 6 to 8 minutes, until squash is fork-tender.

3. Place squash halves, cut side up, on platter. Fill each half with one-fourth of warm bean mixture; sprinkle with tomato and remaining 1 teaspoon chopped sage. Garnish with sage sprigs. Serve with Parmesan, if you like.

**EACH SERVING:** About 250 calories, 9g protein, 47g carbohydrate, 5g total fat (1g saturated), 11g fiber, 0mg cholesterol, 520mg sodium

## IT'S SO GOOD!

Acorn squash offers up a lot of good nutrition. Like its orange veggie brethren the carrot, it is rich in alpha- and beta-carotene, which are the building blocks of vitamin A, as well as supporting antioxidant activity. It's also a good source of vitamin C, potassium, fiber, and omega-3 fatty acids.

# Potato Pancake with Broccoli and Cheddar

*This couldn't be quicker to throw together; if you use already shredded Cheddar, all you have to do is cut any large broccoli flowerets in half. And that little bit of effort turns into a crunchy, cheesy skillet full of goodness.*

**ACTIVE TIME:** 15 minutes | **TOTAL TIME:** 30 minutes

**MAKES:** 4 main-dish servings

1 tablespoon butter or margarine

1 medium onion, chopped

1 bag (12 ounces) broccoli flowerets, each cut in half if large

1 teaspoon salt

2 tablespoons water

4 cups refrigerated shredded hash brown potatoes (one 20-ounce bag or two-thirds 2-pound bag)

⅛ teaspoon ground black pepper

1 tablespoon vegetable oil

4 ounces sharp Cheddar cheese, shredded (1 cup)

1. In nonstick 12-inch skillet, melt butter over medium heat. Add onion and cook until tender, about 8 minutes, stirring frequently. Stir in broccoli, ¼ teaspoon salt, and water; cover and cook until broccoli is tender, about 3 minutes, stirring once. Transfer broccoli mixture to medium bowl.

2. In large bowl, combine potatoes, pepper, and remaining ¾ teaspoon salt. In same skillet, heat oil over medium-high heat until hot. Add half of potato mixture, gently patting with rubber spatula to cover bottom of skillet. Leaving 1-inch border, top potatoes with broccoli mixture. Sprinkle Cheddar over broccoli. Cover cheese with remaining potatoes, patting to edge of skillet. Cook until browned, about 5 minutes.

3. Place large round platter or cookie sheet upside down over skillet. Grasping platter and skillet firmly together, very carefully and quickly flip skillet over to invert pancake onto platter. Slide pancake back into skillet. Cook until other side is browned, about 5 minutes longer. Cut into wedges to serve.

**EACH SERVING:** About 350 calories, 14g protein, 40g carbohydrate, 16g total fat (7g saturated), 5g fiber, 30mg cholesterol, 920mg sodium

# Italian Spinach with Garbanzo Beans and Raisins ⓥ

*This dish is so simple, so delicious, and so good for you. The garbanzo beans provide protein, and the spinach is packed with antioxidants and other nutrients, including bone-building calcium. Enjoy this served over rice.*

**TOTAL TIME:** 15 minutes

**MAKES:** 4 main-dish servings

1 tablespoon olive oil

1 garlic clove, smashed

¼ teaspoon crushed red pepper

1 can (15 to 19 ounces) garbanzo beans, rinsed and drained

2 bunches (10 to 12 ounces each) spinach, tough stems trimmed, washed, and dried very well

¼ cup golden raisins

½ teaspoon salt

## IT'S SO GOOD!

One cup of cooked spinach contains more than 1,000% of the daily recommended requirement for vitamin K and 300% of the requirement for vitamin C. In addition, it contains a cavalcade of bone-building nutrients—calcium, phosphorus, manganese, magnesium, and vitamin A.

1. In 5-quart Dutch oven, heat oil with garlic clove over medium heat until garlic is golden; discard garlic clove. Add crushed red pepper and cook 15 seconds. Stir in garbanzo beans and cook until hot, about 2 minutes, stirring.

2. Increase heat to high. Add spinach, raisins, and salt. Cook just until spinach wilts, 2 to 3 minutes, stirring.

**EACH SERVING:** About 200 calories, 9g protein, 31g carbohydrate, 6g total fat (5g saturated), 9g fiber, 0mg cholesterol, 804mg sodium

# Warm Broccoli and Carrot Slaw

*Kids love this warm vegetable sauté. Add a little fresh lemon juice to brighten the flavor of this healthful side dish.*

**TOTAL TIME:** 10 minutes

**MAKES:** 4 side-dish servings

1 tablespoon butter
1 garlic clove, pressed with garlic press
2 cups shredded broccoli stems
2 cups shredded carrots
salt and ground black pepper

Melt butter in large skillet over medium-high heat. Add garlic, broccoli, and carrots; cook 5 minutes, stirring. Season with salt and pepper.

**EACH SERVING:** About 60 calories, 2g protein, 7g carbohydrate, 3g total fat (0.5g saturated), 3g fiber, 0mg cholesterol, 75mg sodium

 **MAKE IT VEGAN:** *Substitute stick soy margarine.*

# 6

# Hot from the Oven

This chapter is chock-full of hearty fare that will satisfy your whole family. Take your choice from a half dozen meatless lasagna recipes, including one made with sliced precooked polenta instead of noodles. Or choose from among our many other cheesy-good baked pasta dishes.

A great way to get your vegetables is to cook them up in a tasty gratin; we've included one with broccoli and another with spinach. Or enjoy your veggies roasted and stuffed to the brim–you'll find recipes for portobello mushrooms, zucchini halves, and artichokes stuffed with veggies, grains, or some delectable combination.

Casseroles truly are the backbone of family cooking. Ours require a minimum of prep and then it's walk-away time while the casserole cooks into bubbly deliciousness in the oven. We've got a selection your family is going to love, from reinvented Mexican favorites like Nacho Casserole and Chiles Relleños Pie to homey dishes like Vegetable Cobbler and Broccoli-Noodle Casserole. And remember, it takes only a few more minutes to double a recipe and have an extra pan at the ready in the freezer. For tips on freezing and reheating baked pasta dishes and other casseroles, see page 166.

*Clockwise from top left: Spinach and Potato Gratin (page 168); Macaroni and Cheese Deluxe (page 158); Nacho Casserole (page 165); Broccoli Gratin (page 172)*

# Vegetarian Lasagna

*This satisfying pasta dish is overflowing with mushrooms, zucchini, spinach, herbs, and cheese. To get a headstart, prepare the lasagna through Step 4, cover it, and refrigerate overnight. Just pop it in the oven and you've got a delicious dinner on the table in less than 45 minutes.*

**ACTIVE TIME:** 45 minutes
**TOTAL TIME:** 1 hour 10 minutes

**MAKES:** 16 main-dish servings

- 9 lasagna noodles (about half a 16-ounce package)
- 1 tablespoon olive oil
- 1 medium onion, finely chopped
- 8 ounces mushrooms, thinly sliced
- 2 medium zucchini (8 to 10 ounces each), sliced ¼ inch thick
- 1 bunch (8 ounces) spinach, tough stems trimmed
- 2 ripe plum tomatoes, finely chopped
- 2 garlic cloves, minced
- 2 tablespoons chopped fresh parsley
- 2 tablespoons chopped fresh basil
- ½ teaspoon salt
- ½ teaspoon coarsely ground black pepper
- 1 container (15 ounces) part-skim ricotta cheese
- 8 ounces part-skim mozzarella cheese, shredded (2 cups)
- ¼ cup freshly grated Parmesan cheese
- ¼ cup low-fat milk (1%)
- ⅛ teaspoon ground nutmeg
- ¾ cup marinara or other pasta sauce

**1.** In saucepot, cook lasagna noodles as label directs. Drain noodles and rinse with cold running water to stop cooking; drain again. Layer noodles between sheets of waxed paper.

**2.** Meanwhile, in nonstick 12-inch skillet, heat oil over medium-high heat until hot. Add onion and mushrooms, and cook 5 minutes, stirring often. Add zucchini and cook 4 minutes, stirring often. Add spinach and tomatoes, and cook until spinach wilts, vegetables are tender, and most liquid in skillet evaporates, 2 to 3 minutes, stirring often. Stir in garlic, parsley, basil, ¼ teaspoon salt, and ¼ teaspoon pepper; cook 30 seconds, stirring. Set vegetable mixture aside.

**3.** In medium bowl, mix ricotta, mozzarella, Parmesan, milk, nutmeg, remaining ¼ teaspoon salt, and remaining ¼ teaspoon pepper until blended.

**4.** Preheat oven to 425°F. Spoon 1 cup vegetable mixture evenly into 13" by 9" glass baking dish. Arrange 3 noodles over vegetables; evenly spread 1½ cups cheese mixture over noodles and top with 3 noodles. Evenly spoon remaining vegetable mixture over noodles and top with 3 noodles. Evenly spread remaining cheese mixture over noodles; top with marinara sauce.

**5.** Bake lasagna 25 to 30 minutes (35 to 40 minutes if cold) until hot and bubbly. Let lasagna stand 10 minutes for easier serving.

**EACH SERVING:** About 165 calories, 10g protein, 17g carbohydrate, 7g total fat (3g saturated), 2g fiber, 18mg cholesterol, 300mg sodium

# Ratatouille Lasagna

*What a delicious idea, taking ratatouille — that savory combination of peppers, eggplant, and zucchini — and layering it with noodles and Fontina cheese for a lasagna with the taste of Provence!*

**ACTIVE TIME:** 45 minutes
**TOTAL TIME:** 1 hour 45 minutes
**MAKES:** 10 main-dish servings

  1 large green pepper (8 to 10 ounces)
  1 large red pepper (8 to 10 ounces)
  1 small eggplant (1 to 1 ¼ pounds)
  2 small zucchini (6 ounces each)
  4 tablespoons olive or vegetable oil
  2¼ teaspoon salt
  ½ cup water
  1 package (16 ounces) lasagna noodles
  1 medium onion, chopped
  1 can (35 ounces) plum tomatoes
  ½ teaspoon dried thyme
  1 pound Fontina or mozzarella cheese, shredded (4 cups)

1. Cut green and red peppers, eggplant, and zucchini into ¾-inch pieces. In 12-inch skillet heat 3 tablespoons oil over medium-high heat until hot. Add peppers and cook until tender-crisp. Stir in eggplant, zucchini, 1 teaspoon salt, and water; heat to boiling over high heat. Reduce heat to low; cover and simmer until vegetables are tender, about 15 minutes. Remove cover and cook vegetables over high heat until any liquid evaporates, about 5 minutes longer.

2. Meanwhile, prepare lasagna noodles as label directs but do not add salt to water; drain.

3. Prepare sauce: In 4-quart saucepan, heat remaining 1 tablespoon oil over medium heat until hot. Add onion and cook until very tender. Add tomatoes with their juice, thyme, and remaining 1¼ teaspoons salt, breaking tomatoes up with side of spoon; heat to boiling over high heat. Reduce heat to medium; cook 15 minutes.

4. Preheat oven to 375°F. In 13" by 9" glass or ceramic baking dish, arrange one-fourth of lasagna noodles, overlapping to fit. Spread one-third of vegetable mixture over noodles; spoon one-fourth of tomato sauce over vegetables; sprinkle with one-fourth of Fontina. Repeat layering twice. Top with remaining noodles, sauce, and cheese.

5. Bake until lasagna is hot and bubbly and top is lightly browned, about 40 minutes. Remove lasagna from oven; let stand 10 minutes for easier serving.

**EACH SERVING:** About 445 calories, 19g protein, 49g carbohydrate, 20g total fat (9g saturated), 5g fiber, 50mg cholesterol, 1,090mg sodium

# Speedy Vegetable Lasagna

*Who knew lasagna could be this fast and still be so good?*

**ACTIVE TIME:** 30 minutes
**TOTAL TIME:** 1 hour 15 minutes
**MAKES:** 8 main-dish servings

- 1 tablespoon garlic-flavored oil
- 1 large zucchini, thinly sliced
- ½ shredded carrot
- 1 container (15 ounces) part-skim ricotta cheese
- ¾ cup freshly grated Parmesan cheese
- 2 containers (15 ounces each) fat-free refrigerated tomato sauce
- 1 package (10 ounces) frozen chopped spinach, thawed and squeezed dry
- 8 ounces part-skim mozzarella cheese, shredded (2 cups)
- 12 no-boil lasagna noodles (from 8- to 9-ounce package)

1. Preheat oven to 375°F.

2. In a 10-inch skillet, heat oil over medium-high heat until hot. Add zucchini and carrot and cook until vegetables are crisp-tender, about 2 minutes, stirring constantly. Remove to a plate.

3. In a small bowl, stir together ricotta and ½ cup Parmesan.

4. Spread ½ cup tomato sauce in the bottom of a 13" by 9" baking dish. Top with 3 noodles. Spread one-half ricotta mixture over noodles. Sprinkle with half of spinach. Top with 3 noodles. Spread ½ cup sauce. Top with zucchini and carrot, spreading evenly. Sprinkle with 1 cup mozzarella. Spread ½ cup sauce. Top with 3 noodles, remaining ricotta, remaining spinach, ¾ cup sauce, remaining noodles, and remaining sauce. Cover loosely with foil.

5. Bake lasagna 25 minutes. Uncover and sprinkle with remaining 1 cup mozzarella and ¼ cup Parmesan. Bake until bubbly and cheese is melted, about 20 minutes longer. Let stand 10 minutes before cutting.

**EACH SERVING:** About 370 calories, 24g protein, 37g carbohydrate, 15g total fat (8g saturated), 2g fiber, 40mg cholesterol, 440mg sodium

# Three-Cheese Lasagna Rolls

*These roll-ups are served with a quick tomato sauce and zesty zucchini-and-caper topping.*

**ACTIVE TIME:** 25 minutes
**TOTAL TIME:** 1 hour 10 minutes
**MAKES:** 6 main-dish servings

½ package (16-ounce) curly lasagna noodles

2 cans (14½ ounces each) stewed tomatoes

1 can (8 ounces) tomato sauce

1 container (15 ounces) part-skim ricotta cheese

6 ounces part-skim mozzarella cheese, shredded (1½ cups)

3 tablespoons freshly grated Parmesan cheese

½ teaspoon coarsely ground black pepper

4 tablespoons chopped fresh basil

2 teaspoons olive oil

1 small onion, chopped

1 small zucchini (6 ounces), diced

1 small ripe tomato (4 ounces), diced

1 tablespoon capers, drained and chopped

1. Prepare lasagna noodles as label directs. Drain and rinse with cold running water to stop cooking. Return noodles to saucepot with cold water to cover.

2. Meanwhile, in 3-quart glass or ceramic baking dish, combine stewed tomatoes with their juice and tomato sauce, breaking up tomatoes with side of spoon.

3. In large bowl, mix ricotta, mozzarella, Parmesan, pepper, and 3 tablespoons basil.

4. Preheat oven to 375°F.

5. Drain lasagna noodles on clean kitchen towels. Spread rounded ¼ cup cheese filling over each lasagna noodle and roll up jelly-roll fashion. Slice each rolled noodle crosswise in half. Arrange lasagna rolls, cut side down, in sauce in baking dish; cover loosely with foil. Bake until hot, 35 to 40 minutes.

6. Meanwhile, prepare topping: In nonstick 10-inch skillet, heat oil over medium heat until hot. Add onion and cook until tender and browned. Add zucchini and cook until tender. Stir in diced tomato, capers, and remaining 1 tablespoon basil; heat through.

7. To serve, place tomato sauce and lasagna rolls on 6 plates and spoon zucchini topping over lasagna rolls.

**EACH SERVING:** About 385 calories, 24g protein, 43g carbohydrate, 14g total fat (7g saturated), 4g fiber, 40mg cholesterol, 910mg sodium

# Polenta Lasagna

*This stress-free dish is perfect for a last-minute get-together; serve it with mixed baby greens.*

**ACTIVE TIME:** 45 minutes
**TOTAL TIME:** 1 hour 15 minutes
**MAKES:** 6 main-dish servings

1 tablespoon olive oil

1 small onion, finely chopped

1 garlic clove, minced

1 can (28 ounces) tomatoes

2 tablespoons tomato paste

2 tablespoons chopped fresh basil

1 teaspoon salt

1 package (10 ounces) frozen chopped spinach, thawed and squeezed dry

1 cup part-skim ricotta cheese

2 tablespoons freshly grated Parmesan cheese

¼ teaspoon coarsely ground black pepper

1 log (24 ounces) precooked plain polenta, cut into 16 slices

4 ounces part-skim mozzarella cheese, shredded (1 cup)

1. In 3-quart saucepan, heat oil over medium heat until hot. Add onion and cook until tender, about 8 minutes, stirring occasionally. Add garlic and cook 30 seconds longer. Stir in tomatoes with their juice, tomato paste, basil, and ½ teaspoon salt, breaking up tomatoes with side of spoon; heat to boiling over high heat. Reduce heat to low and simmer 20 minutes, stirring occasionally. Set sauce aside.

2. Meanwhile, in medium bowl, mix spinach, ricotta, Parmesan, pepper, and remaining ½ teaspoon salt until blended.

3. Preheat oven to 350°F. Grease 8-inch square glass baking dish.

4. Arrange half of polenta slices, overlapping slightly, in baking dish. Drop half of spinach mixture, by rounded tablespoons, on top of polenta (mixture will not completely cover slices). Pour half of sauce over spinach mixture; spread to form an even layer. Sprinkle with half of mozzarella. Repeat layering.

5. Bake casserole until hot and bubbly, about 30 minutes. Let stand 10 minutes for easier serving.

**EACH SERVING:** About 270 calories, 16g protein, 3g carbohydrate, 10g total fat (1.5g saturated), 4g fiber, 28mg cholesterol, 1,210mg sodium

# Pasta with Roasted Vegetables

*Roasting brings out the naturally delicious flavor of cauliflower and red peppers. If you can't find ricotta salata, shredded Fontina or mozzarella would work well, too.*

**ACTIVE TIME:** 40 minutes
**TOTAL TIME:** 1 hour 35 minutes
**MAKES:** 6 main-dish servings

3 large red peppers (8 to 10 ounces each), cut into 1-inch pieces

4 garlic cloves, peeled

2 tablespoons olive oil

½ teaspoon salt

1 large head cauliflower (2½ pounds), separated into 1-inch flowerets and larger pieces cut into 1-inch pieces

12 ounces cavatelli or bow-tie pasta

1 tablespoon cornstarch

1 can (14½ ounces) vegetable broth

½ cup cold water

⅓ cup loosely packed fresh parsley leaves, chopped

3 tablespoons freshly grated Parmesan cheese

¼ teaspoon ground red pepper (cayenne)

⅛ teaspoon dried thyme

4 ounces ricotta salata cheese, crumbled (1 cup)

1. Preheat oven to 450°F. In 15½" by 10½" jelly-roll pan, toss red-pepper pieces and garlic with 1 tablespoon oil and ¼ teaspoon salt. In another 15½" by 10½" jelly-roll pan or on a large cookie sheet, toss cauliflower pieces with remaining 1 tablespoon oil and remaining ¼ teaspoon salt.

2. Place pans on 2 oven racks in oven. Roast vegetables until browned, about 30 minutes, stirring halfway through roasting time and rotating pans between upper and lower racks after 15 minutes. Turn oven control to 400°F.

3. Meanwhile, in large saucepot, cook pasta as label directs.

4. In 2-quart saucepan, with wire whisk, mix cornstarch with broth and water until blended; heat to boiling over medium-high heat. Boil 1 minute.

5. Drain pasta and return to saucepot. Toss pasta with roasted vegetables, broth mixture, parsley, Parmesan, ground red pepper, and thyme.

6. Transfer pasta to deep 2½-quart baking pan or casserole. Bake pasta 15 minutes.

7. Remove pan from oven and top with ricotta salata. Bake until hot, about 5 minutes longer.

**EACH SERVING:** About 600 calories, 23g protein, 81g carbohydrate, 17g total fat (7g saturated), 2g fiber, 29mg cholesterol, 1,120mg sodium

## IT'S SO GOOD!

One cup cooked cauliflower is packed with cancer-fighting compounds, as well as being an excellent source of vitamins C and K.

# Broccoli and Cheese Manicotti

*Here's a great way to get your kids to eat their broccoli — mix it into the cheesy good filling of manicotti.*

**ACTIVE TIME:** 40 minutes
**TOTAL TIME:** 1 hour 15 minutes
**MAKES:** 6 main-dish servings

- 1 package (12 ounces) medium mushrooms
- 2 small ripe tomatoes (4 ounces each)
- 1 medium onion, peeled
- 2 tablespoons vegetable oil
- 2 packages (10 ounces each) frozen chopped broccoli, thawed and squeezed dry
- 1 container (15 ounces) part-skim ricotta cheese
- 3 ounces mozzarella cheese, shredded (¾ cup)
- ¼ cup freshly grated Parmesan cheese
- ¼ teaspoon ground black pepper
- 2¼ teaspoons salt
- 12 manicotti shells (about one 8-ounce package)
- 1 jar (14 ounces) marinara or spaghetti sauce
- ¾ cup water

1. Thinly slice mushrooms and tomatoes. Chop onion.

2. In 10-inch skillet, heat 1 tablespoon oil over medium heat until hot. Add onion and cook until tender and lightly browned. Remove onion to large bowl; stir in 1½ packages broccoli, ricotta, mozzarella, Parmesan, pepper, and 1¼ teaspoons salt; set aside.

3. Prepare manicotti shells as label directs, adding remaining 1 teaspoon salt in water; drain. Rinse cooked manicotti shells immediately with warm running water to stop the cooking; drain again.

4. Meanwhile, preheat oven to 375°F.

5. In same skillet, heat remaining 1 tablespoon oil over high heat until hot. Add mushrooms and cook until tender; stir in marinara sauce, remaining broccoli, and water; heat through.

6. Using large decorating bag without tube or small spoon, fill manicotti shells with ricotta mixture. Reserve 1 cup marinara sauce. Spoon remaining marinara sauce into 13" by 9" glass baking dish. Arrange filled manicotti shells in sauce in single layer. Tuck tomato slices among manicotti. Spoon reserved marinara sauce over manicotti.

7. Cover dish with foil and bake until hot and bubbly, 25 to 30 minutes. Let stand 10 minutes for easier serving.

**EACH SERVING:** About 445 calories, 24g protein, 52g carbohydrate, 17g total fat (7g saturated), 7g fiber, 37mg cholesterol, 1,160mg sodium

# Baked Penne and Peas

*This satisfying pasta dish is split between two pans. It's perfect if you're serving a crowd (keep one on the table and the other, ready to serve, in the oven), or you can serve one to your family and have the other on call in the freezer.*

*If you want, prepare this dish a day ahead, cover, and refrigerate. When ready to bake, cook until hot and bubbly, 35 to 40 minutes, covering it with foil if the top browns too quickly.*

**ACTIVE TIME:** 45 minutes
**TOTAL TIME:** 1 hour 5 minutes
**MAKES:** 2 pans or 24 main-dish servings

- 2 packages (16 ounces each) penne or ziti pasta
- ¼ cup (½ stick) butter or margarine
- 1 large onion, chopped
- 2 garlic cloves, crushed with garlic press
- 2 cans (14½ ounces each) diced tomatoes
- 1 cup packed fresh basil leaves, chopped
- 2 teaspoons salt
- ½ teaspoon ground black pepper
- 3 tablespoons cornstarch
- 5 cups whole milk
- 1 cup heavy or whipping cream
- 2 cups freshly grated Parmesan cheese (8 ounces)
- 1 bag (20 ounces) frozen peas

## IT'S SO GOOD!

Most kids love peas and it's good to know they supply important nutrients like bone-building manganese, phosphorus, and magnesium, immune system-supporting vitamin A and zinc, as well as protein and iron.

1. In 12-quart saucepot, cook pasta as label directs, but just until al dente.

2. Meanwhile, in 5- to 6-quart saucepot, melt butter over medium heat. Add onion and cook until tender and golden, 10 to 12 minutes, stirring occasionally. Add garlic and cook 1 minute, stirring. Add tomatoes with their juice, basil, salt, and pepper; heat to boiling. Reduce heat to medium-low and simmer 5 minutes, stirring occasionally.

3. In cup, with wire whisk or fork, mix cornstarch and ½ cup milk until blended. Pour cornstarch mixture, cream, 1 cup Parmesan, and remaining 4½ cups milk into tomato mixture; heat to boiling over medium-high heat. Boil until sauce thickens, about 1 minute, stirring often; set aside.

4. Preheat oven to 400°F. Place frozen peas in large colander and drain pasta over peas. Return pasta mixture to 12-quart saucepot. Stir sauce into pasta mixture until combined.

5. Spoon pasta mixture into 2 shallow 3½- to 4-quart glass or ceramic casseroles or two 13" by 9" glass baking dishes. Sprinkle ½ cup Parmesan on top of each casserole. Bake casseroles until hot and bubbly, about 20 minutes.

**EACH SERVING:** About 300 calories, 12g protein, 39g carbohydrate, 11g total fat (5g saturated), 3g fiber, 27mg cholesterol, 615mg sodium

# Ziti with Eggplant and Ricotta

*If you want to prepare this dish ahead, roast the eggplant, make the sauce, and refrigerate separately. When ready to bake, cook the pasta and assemble; add about 10 minutes to the baking time to compensate for the chilled ingredients.*

**ACTIVE TIME:** 40 minutes | **TOTAL TIME:** 1 hour

**MAKES:** 6 main-dish servings

- 1 medium eggplant (1½ to 2 pounds), cut into 1-inch pieces
- 3 tablespoons olive oil
- ¾ teaspoon salt
- 1 small onion, finely chopped
- 2 garlic cloves, minced
- 1 can (28 ounces) plum tomatoes
- 2 tablespoons tomato paste
- ¼ teaspoon ground black pepper
- 3 tablespoons chopped fresh basil
- 1 package (16 ounces) ziti or penne pasta
- ¼ cup freshly grated Parmesan cheese
- 1 cup ricotta cheese

1. Preheat oven to 450°F. In large bowl, toss eggplant, 2 tablespoons oil, and ¼ teaspoon salt until evenly coated. Arrange eggplant in single layer in two 15½" by 10½" jelly-roll pans or 2 large baking sheets. Place pans on 2 oven racks in oven. Roast eggplant until tender and golden, about 30 minutes, rotating pans between upper and lower racks halfway through cooking and stirring twice. Remove pans from oven; set aside. Turn oven control to 400°F.

2. Meanwhile, in 3-quart saucepan, heat remaining 1 tablespoon oil over medium heat until hot. Add onion and cook until tender, about 5 minutes, stirring occasionally. Add garlic and cook 1 minute longer, stirring frequently. Stir in tomatoes with their juice, tomato paste, pepper, and remaining ½ teaspoon salt, breaking up tomatoes with side of spoon; heat to boiling over high heat. Reduce heat to low and simmer until sauce thickens slightly, about 10 minutes. Stir in 2 tablespoons basil.

3. In large saucepot, prepare pasta as label directs. Drain; return pasta to saucepot.

4. To pasta in saucepot, add roasted eggplant, tomato sauce, and Parmesan; toss until evenly mixed. Spoon mixture into six 2-cup gratin dishes or shallow casseroles; top with dollops of ricotta. Cover casseroles with foil and bake until hot and bubbly, about 20 minutes.

5. To serve, sprinkle tops with remaining 1 tablespoon basil.

**EACH SERVING:** About 500 calories, 19g protein, 73g carbohydrate, 15g total fat (5g saturated), 2g fiber, 24mg cholesterol, 695mg sodium

# Macaroni and Cheese Deluxe

*This dish is filled with the sophisticated flavors of blue cheese, fragrant toasted nuts, and Parmesan-dusted tomatoes. It's perfect for a weekend dinner party.*

**ACTIVE TIME:** 40 minutes | **TOTAL TIME:** 1 hour

**MAKES:** 6 main-dish servings

1 package (16 ounces) campanelle or penne pasta

3 tablespoons butter or margarine

1 medium onion, diced

2 tablespoons all-purpose flour

¼ teaspoon salt

¼ teaspoon coarsely ground black pepper

¼ teaspoon ground red pepper (cayenne)

¼ teaspoon ground nutmeg

4 cups low-fat milk (1%)

½ cup freshly grated Parmesan cheese

1 cup frozen peas

4 ounces creamy blue cheese (like Gorgonzola), cut up or crumbled into pieces

½ pint pear-shaped or round cherry tomatoes, each cut in half

½ cup walnuts, toasted (see Cook's Tip, page 63)

1. In large saucepot, prepare pasta as label directs. Preheat oven to 400°F.

2. Meanwhile, in deep 3-quart saucepan, melt butter over medium heat; add onion and cook until tender, about 8 minutes, stirring occasionally. With wire whisk, stir in flour, salt, black pepper, ground red pepper, and nutmeg, and cook 1 minute, stirring constantly.

3. Gradually whisk in milk and cook over medium-high heat, stirring frequently, until sauce boils and thickens slightly. Boil 1 minute, stirring. Stir in ¼ cup Parmesan. Remove casserole from heat.

4. Place frozen peas in colander; drain pasta over peas and return pasta mixture to saucepot. Stir in sauce and blue cheese. Transfer pasta mixture to saucepan.

5. In small bowl, toss tomato halves with remaining ¼ cup Parmesan. Top casserole with tomato halves. Bake until casserole is hot and bubbly and top is lightly browned, about 20 minutes.

6. Sprinkle with toasted walnuts before serving.

**EACH SERVING:** About 610 calories, 26g protein, 76g carbohydrate, 23g total fat (6g saturated), 5g fiber, 43mg cholesterol, 965mg sodium

# Baked Ziti and Vegetables

*Chock-full of caramelized vegetables, you won't even miss the sausage and meatballs in this meatless version of baked ziti.*

**ACTIVE TIME:** 20 minutes | **TOTAL TIME:** 1 hour
**MAKES:** 6 main-dish servings

1 package (16 ounces) ziti or penne macaroni

2 medium green peppers (4 to 6 ounces each)

2 medium carrots, peeled

2 medium stalks celery

1 medium onion, peeled

1 tablespoon vegetable oil

¼ cup water

1 can (28 ounces) crushed tomatoes

3 cups spicy hot juice or vegetable juice

1 tablespoon sugar

1½ teaspoons salt

½ teaspoon dried oregano

8 ounces reduced-fat mozzarella cheese, shredded (2 cups)

2 tablespoons freshly grated Parmesan cheese

1. In saucepot, prepare ziti as label directs.

2. Meanwhile, cut green peppers, carrots, celery, and onion into ½-inch pieces. In nonstick 12-inch skillet, heat oil over medium-high heat until hot. Add vegetables and cook until lightly browned.

3. Stir in water; continue cooking over medium heat until vegetables are tender-crisp.

4. Preheat oven to 375°F.

5. Drain ziti in colander; set aside. To same saucepot, add cooked vegetables; stir in tomatoes, juice, sugar, salt, and oregano; heat to boiling over high heat. Remove saucepot from heat; stir in ziti.

6. Reserve 1 cup mozzarella for topping. Into ziti mixture in saucepot, stir Parmesan and remaining mozzarella. Spoon mixture into shallow 4-quart casserole; sprinkle with reserved mozzarella. Cover casserole and bake until mozzarella melts and mixture is hot and bubbly, about 30 minutes.

**EACH SERVING:** About 490 calories, 25g protein, 82g carbohydrate, 8g total fat (3g saturated), 8g fiber, 15mg cholesterol, 1,430mg sodium

# Easy Ravioli Casserole

*Your kids won't even know they're eating their vegetables (they're hidden in the tomato sauce!).*

**ACTIVE TIME:** 20 minutes | **TOTAL TIME:** 1 hour
**MAKES:** 6 main-dish servings

1 small eggplant (1 to 1¼ pounds)
1 medium stalk celery
1 medium carrot, peeled
1 small onion, peeled
3 tablespoons olive oil
1 can (28 ounces) plum tomatoes
½ teaspoon sugar
½ teaspoon salt
2 packages (13 ounces each) frozen large cheese ravioli
8 ounces part-skim mozzarella cheese, shredded (2 cups)

1. Dice eggplant. Finely chop celery, carrot, and onion. In 4-quart saucepan, heat oil over medium heat until very hot. Add eggplant, celery, carrot, and onion; cover and cook until vegetables are almost tender, 8 to 10 minutes, stirring occasionally. Stir in tomatoes with their juice, sugar, and salt; heat to boiling over high heat. Reduce heat to low; cover and simmer 15 minutes, breaking up tomatoes with side of spoon.

2. Preheat oven to 375°F. Meanwhile, prepare ravioli as label directs; drain.

3. Into 13" by 9" glass baking dish, spoon 1½ cups tomato sauce. Top with half of ravioli, half of remaining sauce, and half of mozzarella. Repeat layers. Bake until casserole is bubbly and cheese on top is golden, about 30 minutes.

**EACH SERVING:** About 460 calories, 24g protein, 44g carbohydrate, 22g total fat (10g saturated), 5g fiber, 50mg cholesterol, 1,004mg sodium

## TO FREEZE AND REHEAT CASSEROLES

Cool casserole 30 minutes at room temperature, then place in refrigerator to cool 30 minutes longer. When cool, wrap baking dish tightly with heavy-duty foil or several layers of plastic wrap; label and freeze up to 3 months.

Up to 2 days before serving, place frozen casserole in refrigerator to thaw slightly. When ready to serve, preheat oven to 350°F. Unwrap casserole; bake, covered loosely with foil, about 1 hour. Remove foil and bake 20 to 30 minutes longer, or until heated through and internal temperature on instant-read thermometer reaches 165°F.

Or, unwrap slightly thawed casserole and place in microwave oven. Cover with waxed paper and heat on Defrost until knife can be easily inserted in center. Then heat on High until temperature reaches 165°F.

**TIP:** To avoid tying up a casserole dish in the freezer for weeks, line your casserole dish with heavy-duty foil before you fill it with casserole mixture or lasagna. Freeze in dish until solid, then transfer frozen casserole with foil into a self-sealing plastic bag; return to freezer. When you're ready to bake, unwrap the frozen block and slip it back into its original dish.

# Spinach and Ricotta Dumplings

*Fluffy ricotta and spinach dumplings, a light version of gnocchi, are served up in a creamy white sauce with a generous sprinkling of Parmesan.*

**ACTIVE TIME:** 45 minutes | **TOTAL TIME:** 1 hour

**MAKES:** 4 main-dish servings

- 2 bunches (10 ounces each) spinach, or 2 packages (10 ounces each) frozen spinach, thawed
- 1 cup ricotta cheese
- 2 large eggs
- ½ teaspoon salt
- ¼ teaspoon ground black pepper
- 1 cup freshly grated Parmesan cheese (4 ounces)
- ½ cup plus 2 tablespoons all-purpose flour
- 2 tablespoons butter or margarine
- 2 cups milk

1. If using fresh spinach, trim tough stems and wash spinach well. In 5-quart Dutch oven, cook spinach with water clinging to leaves over high heat, stirring, just until wilted. Drain. Squeeze dry; coarsely chop.

2. Prepare dumplings: In large bowl, mix spinach, ricotta, eggs, salt, pepper, ½ cup Parmesan, and ½ cup flour. With floured hands, shape spinach mixture into 2" by 1" ovals.

3. Meanwhile, fill 5-quart saucepot halfway with water. Heat to boiling over high heat. Reduce heat to medium. Add dumplings, half at a time. Cook dumplings in simmering water until they float to the top, 3 to 5 minutes, gently stirring occasionally. With slotted spoon, transfer dumplings to paper towels to drain.

4. Preheat oven to 350°F.

5. Prepare white sauce: In 2-quart saucepan, melt butter over medium heat. Stir in remaining 2 tablespoons flour; cook 1 minute. Gradually whisk in milk and cook, whisking constantly, until sauce boils and thickens slightly. Remove saucepan from heat; stir in ¼ cup Parmesan.

6. Place dumplings in single layer in shallow 2-quart casserole; spoon sauce on top. Sprinkle remaining ¼ cup Parmesan over top. Bake until sauce is hot and bubbly, 15 to 20 minutes.

**EACH SERVING:** About 445 calories, 28g protein, 27g carbohydrate, 26g total fat (13g saturated), 3g fiber, 167mg cholesterol, 860mg sodium

# Vegetable Potpies with Curry Crust

*Here's a vegetarian spin on the chicken classic. The filling is sparked with the flavors of cilantro and mango chutney; it's topped with a curry-scented pastry crust.*

**ACTIVE TIME:** 1 hour 15 minutes
**TOTAL TIME:** 1 hour 40 minutes

**MAKES:** 4 main-dish servings

2 teaspoons curry powder

½ teaspoon salt

1¼ cups plus 2 tablespoons all-purpose flour

2 tablespoons vegetable shortening

6 tablespoons butter or margarine

3 tablespoons cold water, or as needed

1 can (14½ ounces) vegetable broth

3 medium carrots, peeled and cut into ½-inch-thick slices

1 medium sweet potato, peeled and cut into 1-inch pieces

1 medium onion, diced

1 teaspoon mustard seeds

½ teaspoon ground cumin

½ teaspoon ground coriander

1 can (15 to 19 ounces) garbanzo beans, rinsed and drained

2 tablespoons mango chutney, chopped

**1.** In medium bowl, combine curry powder, salt, and 1¼ cups flour. With pastry blender or two knives used scissor-fashion, cut in shortening and 4 tablespoons butter until mixture resembles coarse crumbs. Sprinkle cold water, 1 tablespoon at a time, into flour mixture, mixing with fork after each addition until dough is just moist enough to hold together. Shape dough into a disk; wrap and refrigerate 30 minutes.

**2.** Meanwhile, in 2-quart saucepan, heat broth, carrots, and sweet potato to boiling over high heat. Reduce heat to low; cover and simmer until vegetables are tender, about 10 minutes. Strain broth into 4-cup glass measuring cup or medium bowl. Transfer vegetable mixture to large bowl.

**3.** In same saucepan, melt 1 tablespoon butter over medium heat. Add onion and cook until tender, about 8 minutes, stirring. Stir in mustard seeds, cumin, and coriander; cook 2 minutes longer, stirring. Transfer onion mixture to bowl with vegetables.

**4.** Preheat oven to 425°F.

**5.** In same saucepan, melt remaining 1 tablespoon butter over medium heat. Add remaining 2 tablespoons flour and cook, whisking, until golden, 1 to 2 minutes. Gradually stir in reserved broth; cook, whisking, until mixture boils and thickens slightly. Stir broth, garbanzo beans, and chutney into vegetable in bowl. Spoon vegetable mixture into 4 deep 1½-cup ramekins or soufflé dishes.

**6.** Divide chilled dough into quarters. On lightly floured surface, with floured rolling pin, roll 1 piece of dough ¾ inch larger in diameter than top of ramekin. With small cookie cutter or tip of knife, cut out design near center of dough to allow steam to escape during baking. Place dough on top of ramekin; fold edge over side of ramekin and press lightly to seal. Repeat with remaining dough.

**7.** Place filled ramekins on cookie sheet and to catch any drips during baking. Bake potpies until crusts are lightly browned and filling is hot and bubbly, about 25 minutes.

EACH SERVING: About 625 calories, 15g protein, 86g carbohydrate, 28g total fat (7g saturated), 10g fiber, Omg cholesterol, 1,170mg sodium

# Vegetarian Tortilla Pie

*This dish can be assembled in a jiffy, thanks to its no-cook filling of canned black beans and corn, prepared salsa, and pre-shredded Jack cheese. A wedge of iceberg lettuce on the side topped with your choice of dressing will provide the missing crunch.*

ACTIVE TIME: 20 minutes | TOTAL TIME: 30 minutes
MAKES: 4 main-dish servings

1 jar (11 to 12 ounces) medium salsa
1 can (8 ounces) no-salt-added tomato sauce
1 can (15 to 16 ounces) no-salt-added black beans, rinsed and drained
1 can (15¼ ounces) no-salt-added whole-kernel corn, drained
½ cup packed fresh cilantro leaves
4 (10-inch) low-fat flour tortillas
6 ounces reduced-fat Monterey Jack cheese, shredded (1½ cups)
reduced-fat sour cream (optional)

**1.** Preheat oven to 500°F. Spray 15½" by 10½" jelly-roll pan with nonstick cooking spray.

**2.** In small bowl, mix salsa and tomato sauce. In medium bowl, mix black beans, corn, and cilantro.

**3.** Place 1 tortilla in jelly-roll pan. Spread one-third of salsa mixture over tortilla. Top with one-third of bean mixture and one-third of Monterey Jack. Repeat layering two more times, ending with last tortilla.

**4.** Bake pie until cheese melts and filling is hot, 10 to 12 minutes. Serve with sour cream, if you like.

EACH SERVING: About 440 calories, 25g protein, 65g carbohydrate, 11g total fat (5g saturated), 13g fiber, 30mg cholesterol, 820mg sodium

# Chiles Relleños Pie

*Stuff canned chiles with store-bought bean dip, place on rice, top with a no-fuss cheese custard—easy as pie!*

**ACTIVE TIME:** 10 minutes | **TOTAL TIME:** 1 hour

**MAKES:** 6 main-dish servings

- ½ cup long-grain rice
- 2 cans (4 ounces each) mild green chiles, rinsed, drained, and patted dry
- ⅔ cup (about half of 11.5- to 12.5-ounce jar) bean dip
- 4 large eggs
- 2 cups milk
- ½ teaspoon salt
- 4 ounces Monterey Jack cheese, shredded (1 cup)

1. Prepare rice as label directs, but do not add salt to water.

2. Meanwhile, with knife, split each chile lengthwise in half, but not all the way through. Spoon 1 heaping tablespoon bean dip onto half of each chile; fold remaining half over.

3. In medium bowl, with wire whisk or fork, mix eggs, milk, and salt until well blended.

4. Preheat oven to 325°F. Spoon cooked rice into shallow 1½-quart casserole or 9½-inch deep-dish pie plate. Place stuffed chiles on top of rice. Pour egg mixture over chiles; sprinkle with Monterey Jack.

5. Bake pie until knife inserted in center comes out clean, about 50 minutes. Cut into wedges.

**EACH SERVING:** About 255 calories, 14g protein, 23g carbohydrate, 12g total fat (6g saturated), 2g fiber, 170mg cholesterol, 795mg sodium

# Corn, Black Bean and Rice Burritos

*These yummy vegetarian baked burritos are jam-packed with a savory mixture of corn, chiles, cheese, black beans, and rice.*

**ACTIVE TIME:** 20 minutes | **TOTAL TIME:** 35 minutes

**MAKES:** 4 main-dish servings

- ¼ package (1 boil-in bag from 14 ounce box) precooked long-grain rice
- 1 can (15 to 19 ounces) black beans, rinsed and drained
- 1 can (15¼ to 16 ounces) whole-kernel corn, drained
- 1 can (4 to 4½ ounces) chopped mild green chiles, drained
- ⅔ cup shredded Monterey Jack or Cheddar cheese
- ¼ cup chopped fresh cilantro
- 8 (6- to 7-inch) low-fat flour tortillas
- 1 jar (12½ ounces) fat-free mild salsa

1. Preheat oven to 425°F. Prepare rice as label directs.

2. Meanwhile, in large bowl, combine black beans, corn, chiles, Monterey Jack, and cilantro.

3. When rice is done, stir into bean mixture. Spoon rounded ½ cup rice mixture along center of each tortilla. Spoon 1 tablespoon salsa on top of rice filling. Fold sides of tortilla over filling, overlapping slightly.

**4.** Spray 13" by 9" glass or ceramic baking dish with nonstick cooking spray. Place burritos, seam-side down, in dish. Spoon any remaining rice mixture in a row down center of burritos; top rice with remaining salsa. Cover loosely with foil and bake 15 minutes.

EACH SERVING: About 525 calories, 24g protein, 98g carbohydrate, 9g total fat (4g saturated),14g fiber, 17mg cholesterol, 1,470mg sodium

 MAKE IT VEGAN: *Omit the Monterey Jack.*

**1.** Preheat oven to 400°F.

**2.** In 13" by 9" ceramic or glass baking dish, stir undiluted soup with milk; spread evenly. Top with half of salsa and half of chips. Carefully spread beans over chips. Top with remaining chips and salsa. Sprinkle with chiles and Cheddar.

**3.** Bake until hot, about 20 minutes.

EACH SERVING: About 385 calories, 17g protein, 60g carbohydrate, 12g total fat (5g saturated), 5g fiber, 27mg cholesterol, 1,370mg sodium

# Nacho Casserole

*Warning: This casserole may become a family favorite! For less "heat," omit the jalapeños.*

ACTIVE TIME: 10 minutes | TOTAL TIME: 30 minutes
MAKES: 6 main-dish servings

1 can (10¾ ounces) condensed Cheddar cheese soup
½ cup low-fat milk (1%)
1 jar (16 ounces) mild or medium-hot salsa
1 bag (7 ounces) unsalted baked tortilla chips
1 can (16 ounces) fat-free refried beans
2 jalapeño chiles, thinly sliced
4 ounces Cheddar cheese, shredded (1 cup)

# Chili Casserole with Cornbread Topping Ⓥ

*A little box of cornbread mix turns black-and-pink-bean chili into something special.*

**ACTIVE TIME:** 40 minutes  |  **TOTAL TIME:** 55 minutes

**MAKES:** 6 main-dish servings

- 1 tablespoon olive oil
- 6 medium carrots, peeled and cut into ¼-inch dice
- 2 medium stalks celery, cut into ¼-inch dice
- 1 large onion, cut into ¼-inch dice
- 2 garlic cloves, minced
- 3 tablespoons chili powder
- 1 teaspoon ground cumin
- 1 can (15 ounces) crushed tomatoes in puree
- 1 can (15 to 19 ounces) black beans, rinsed and drained
- 1 can (15 to 19 ounces) pink beans, rinsed and drained
- 1 package (10 ounces) frozen whole-kernel corn
- 1 cup reduced-sodium vegetable broth
- 1 package (8½ ounces) corn-muffin mix
- ½ cup loosely packed fresh cilantro leaves, chopped

1. Preheat oven to 400°F.

2. In nonstick 12-inch skillet with oven-safe handles (or cover handles with heavy-duty foil for baking in oven later), heat oil over medium heat until hot. Add carrots, celery, and onion; cover and cook until vegetables are tender, about 15 minutes, stirring occasionally.

3. Stir in garlic, chili powder, and cumin; cook 2 minutes, stirring. Stir in tomatoes, black and pink beans, corn, and broth; heat to boiling over high heat. Reduce heat to low; cover and simmer 5 minutes.

4. Meanwhile, prepare corn-muffin mix as label directs.

5. Top hot chili mixture in skillet with corn-muffin batter, leaving 2-inch border. Bake until cornbread is golden and toothpick inserted in center of topping comes out clean, 15 to 20 minutes. Sprinkle with cilantro to serve.

**EACH SERVING:** About 500 calories, 20g protein, 85g carbohydrate, 11g total fat (3g saturated), 14g fiber, 42mg cholesterol, 1,160mg sodium

# Eggplant and Spinach Stacks

*Thick slices of roasted eggplant layered with spinach, zucchini, and cheese is a fun, new way to serve this sometime forgotten vegetable. All you need are hearts of romaine and good bread to complete the meal.*

**ACTIVE TIME:** 25 minutes  |  **TOTAL TIME:** 50 minutes
**MAKES:** 4 main-dish servings

1 medium eggplant (1½ to 2 pounds)
1 tablespoon plus 3 teaspoons olive oil
1 teaspoon salt
2 garlic cloves, crushed with garlic press
⅛ teaspoon crushed red pepper
1 small zucchini (6 ounces), coarsely shredded
1 bag (6 ounces) baby spinach leaves
1 cup part-skim ricotta cheese
¼ cup freshly grated Parmesan cheese
2 ripe plum tomatoes, seeded and cut into paper-thin strips
⅛ teaspoon cracked black pepper
fresh thyme leaves for garnish

1. Preheat oven to 450°F. Cut ends from eggplant and discard. Cut crosswise into 8 rounds of equal thickness. Brush cut sides of eggplant slices with 1 tablespoon plus 2 teaspoons oil. Sprinkle slices with ½ teaspoon salt and place in 15½" by 10½" jelly-roll pan. Roast eggplant slices until tender and golden, 20 to 25 minutes, carefully turning slices over halfway through cooking.

2. Meanwhile, in nonstick 12-inch skillet, heat remaining 1 teaspoon oil over medium heat until hot. Add garlic and crushed red pepper, and cook 30 seconds, stirring. Add zucchini and ¼ teaspoon salt, and cook 2 minutes, stirring. Gradually add spinach to skillet, stirring until wilted and water evaporates, about 3 minutes; set aside.

3. In small bowl, mix ricotta, Parmesan, and remaining ¼ teaspoon salt until blended.

4. Remove pan with eggplant from oven. Mound spinach mixture on 4 of the larger eggplant slices in pan; top with remaining eggplant slices. Mound equal amounts of cheese mixture on each eggplant stack. Return to oven; heat through, about 5 minutes (cheese will melt over side of stacks). With wide metal spatula, transfer stacks to 4 dinner plates; top with tomatoes, sprinkle with black pepper, and garnish with thyme leaves.

**EACH SERVING:** About 230 calories, 13g protein, 17g carbohydrate, 14g total fat (5g saturated), 6g fiber, 23mg cholesterol, 795mg sodium

# Spinach and Potato Gratin

*Serve this with a green salad and some crusty bread and you've got a complete meal.*

**ACTIVE TIME:** 40 minutes
**TOTAL TIME:** 2 hours 10 minutes
**MAKES:** 12 side-dish servings

1 tablespoon butter or margarine

3 large shallots, thinly sliced

2 packages (10 ounces each) frozen chopped spinach, thawed and squeezed dry

½ teaspoon salt

½ teaspoon coarsely ground black pepper

⅛ teaspoon ground nutmeg

3 pounds all-purpose potatoes (9 medium), peeled and cut into ¼-inch-thick slices

4 ounces Gruyère cheese, shredded (1 cup)

1½ cups milk

1 cup heavy or whipping cream

1 tablespoon cornstarch

1. Preheat oven to 350°F. Grease shallow 3-quart casserole.

2. In 10-inch skillet, melt butter over medium heat. Add shallots and cook until tender, about 5 minutes, stirring occasionally. Remove skillet from heat; stir in spinach, ¼ teaspoon salt, ¼ teaspoon pepper, and nutmeg.

3. Arrange one-third of potato slices, overlapping, in prepared casserole. Top with one-third of Gruyère and one-half of spinach mixture. Repeat layering with remaining ingredients, ending with Gruyère.

4. In large bowl, with wire whisk, mix milk, cream, cornstarch, remaining ¼ teaspoon salt, and remaining ¼ teaspoon pepper until smooth. Pour milk mixture evenly over casserole.

5. Place sheet of foil underneath casserole; crimp foil edges to form a rim to catch any drips during baking. Cover casserole and bake 30 minutes. Remove cover and bake until casserole is hot and bubbly and top is golden, about 1 hour longer.

**EACH SERVING:** About 250 calories, 8g protein, 24g carbohydrate, 13g total fat (7g saturated), 3g fiber, 42mg cholesterol, 315mg sodium

# Portobellos with Potato and Swiss Chard

*Thick, meaty mushroom caps are baked until tender, then topped with garlicky greens and mashed potatoes.*

**ACTIVE TIME:** 20 minutes
**TOTAL TIME:** 1 hour 5 minutes
**MAKES:** 4 main-dish servings

    4 tablespoons olive oil
    2 garlic cloves, crushed with garlic press
    1 teaspoon salt
    4 large (4½- to 5-inch) portobello mushrooms (5 ounces each), stems removed
    2 large all-purpose potatoes (1¼ pounds), peeled and cut into 1½-inch chunks
    ¼ teaspoon coarsely ground black pepper
    1 shallot, minced
    1 bunch (12 ounces) Swiss chard, bottom 2 inches of stems trimmed and leaves coarsely chopped
    ¼ cup freshly grated Parmesan cheese

1. Preheat oven to 450°F. In cup, mix 2 tablespoons oil with half of crushed garlic and ¼ teaspoon salt. Place portobello caps in 15½" by 10½" jelly-roll pan stem side up. Brush inside of mushrooms with oil mixture. Add ⅓ cup water to pan; cover with foil and bake until mushrooms are tender, about 45 minutes.

2. Meanwhile, in 3-quart saucepan, place potatoes with enough water to cover; heat to boiling over high heat. Reduce heat to low; cover and simmer until tender, about 15 minutes. Drain potatoes, reserving *½ cup cooking water*. Return potatoes to saucepan; add pepper, remaining ¾ teaspoon salt, and reserved cooking water. With potato masher, mash potatoes until almost smooth.

3. In nonstick 12-inch skillet, heat remaining 2 tablespoons oil over medium heat until hot. Add shallot and cook until tender, about 5 minutes, stirring occasionally. Add remaining garlic, and cook 30 seconds, stirring. Increase heat to medium-high; add Swiss chard, and cook until leaves wilt and stems are tender-crisp, about 5 minutes, stirring occasionally. Stir in mashed potatoes.

4. Spoon one-fourth of potato mixture into each roasted portobello cap; sprinkle with Parmesan and serve.

**EACH SERVING:** About 310 calories, 10g protein, 35g carbohydrate, 15g total fat (3g saturated), 7g fiber, 4mg cholesterol, 840mg sodium

Ⓥ MAKE IT VEGAN: *Omit the Parmesan.*

# Creamy Parmesan Twice-Baked Potatoes

*We microwaved the potatoes and used a Parmesan-peppercorn salad dressing in this easy version of twice-baked potatoes. Reheat the stuffed potatoes in the oven for a crispy top, but if you're short on time, just pop them in the microwave.*

**ACTIVE TIME:** 20 minutes  |  **TOTAL TIME:** 45 minutes

**MAKES:** 4 main-dish servings

> ## IT'S SO GOOD!
>
> Potatoes are rich in complex carbohydrates—an important source of energy. They also supply antioxidants, which stabilize free radicals (preventing them from damaging cells). Spuds pack a healthy dose of fiber, potassium, and vitamin C, particularly if you eat them with their skin.

4 medium baking potatoes (10 ounces each)

½ cup bottled creamy Parmesan with cracked peppercorn salad dressing

1 green onion, thinly sliced

¼ cup freshly grated Parmesan cheese

green-onion tops (optional)

**1.** Pierce potatoes with fork in several places. Place potatoes on paper towel in microwave oven. Cook on High 10 to 12 minutes, until fork-tender, turning potatoes over once halfway through cooking; cool slightly.

**2.** Meanwhile, preheat oven to 450°F. In medium bowl, mix salad dressing and sliced green onion; set aside.

**3.** When potatoes are cool enough to handle, slice each lengthwise in half. With spoon, carefully scoop out flesh from each potato half, leaving ¼-inch-thick shell and making sure potato-skin shells are intact. Place flesh in bowl with dressing mixture. Place shells on small baking sheet.

**4.** With potato masher or fork, mash potato mixture in bowl until almost smooth. Spoon mashed-potato mixture into shells; sprinkle with Parmesan.

**5.** Bake potatoes until heated through and golden on top, 12 to 15 minutes. Arrange potatoes on bed of green-onion tops if you like.

**EACH SERVING:** About 420 calories, 8g protein, 61g carbohydrate, 18g total fat (4g saturated), 5g fiber, 4mg cholesterol, 440mg sodium

**HORSERADISH AND CHEDDAR TWICE-BAKED POTATOES:** Prepare recipe as above, except in step 2, substitute *⅔ cup reduced-fat sour cream* and *¼ cup prepared white horseradish* for salad dressing. In step 4, substitute *½ cup shredded Cheddar cheese* for Parmesan.

**EACH SERVING:** About 370 calories, 10g protein, 62g carbohydrate, 10g total fat (6g saturated), 6g fiber, 30mg cholesterol, 135mg sodium

# Broccoli Gratin

*We've trimmed the fat from a family favorite by using creamy Yukon Gold potatoes as the base of this dish, making the traditional use of heavy cream and milk unnecessary.*

**ACTIVE TIME:** 10 minutes | **TOTAL TIME:** 30 minutes

**MAKES:** 8 side-dish servings

1 pound broccoli flowerets

1 pound Yukon Gold potatoes, peeled and cut into 1-inch chunks

2 cups water

pinch ground nutmeg

¾ cup freshly grated Parmesan cheese

½ teaspoon salt

¼ teaspoon coarsely ground black pepper

**COOK'S TIP**

The unbaked casserole can be refrigerated up to 1 day. Bake 10 minutes longer than directed.

1. In 4-quart saucepan, place broccoli, potatoes, and water. Cover and heat to boiling over high heat. Reduce heat to medium-low; cover and cook until potatoes and broccoli are very tender, 17 to 20 minutes, stirring once halfway through cooking.

2. Meanwhile, preheat broiler and set oven rack 6 inches from source of heat.

3. Drain vegetables in colander set over large bowl, reserving *¼ cup cooking water*. Return vegetables to saucepan. With potato masher or slotted spoon, coarsely mash vegetables, adding some reserved vegetable cooking liquid if mixture seems dry. Stir in nutmeg, ¼ cup Parmesan, salt, and pepper.

4. In shallow, broiler-safe 1- to 1½-quart baking dish, spread vegetable mixture; sprinkle with remaining ½ cup Parmesan. Place dish in oven and broil until Parmesan is browned, 2 to 3 minutes.

**EACH SERVING:** About 95 calories, 6g protein, 13g carbohydrate, 3g total fat (2g saturated), 2g fiber, 6mg cholesterol, 305mg sodium

# Broccoli-Cheddar Puff

*The addition of whipped egg whites gives this dish its "puff." It's both light and satisfying.*

**ACTIVE TIME:** 35 minutes
**TOTAL TIME:** 1 hour 15 minutes
**MAKES:** 15 side-dish servings

5 tablespoons butter or margarine

6 tablespoons all-purpose flour

½ teaspoon salt

⅛ teaspoon ground red pepper (cayenne)

2¼ cups whole milk

8 ounces sharp Cheddar cheese, shredded (2 cups)

2 packages (10 ounces each) frozen chopped broccoli, thawed and squeezed dry

7 large eggs, separated

1½ cups coarse soft fresh bread crumbs (from 3 slices firm white bread)

1. In 4-quart saucepan, melt 4 tablespoons butter over medium-low heat. Stir in flour, salt, and ground red pepper until blended; cook 1 minute, stirring. Gradually stir in milk; cook until mixture boils and thickens, stirring frequently. Stir in Cheddar; cook just until melted. Remove from heat. Stir in broccoli.

2. In small bowl, with fork, lightly beat egg yolks. Stir in about ½ cup cheese sauce. Gradually pour egg-yolk mixture into cheese sauce, stirring rapidly to prevent curdling. Cool slightly.

3. Meanwhile, preheat oven to 325°F. Grease shallow 3½-quart ceramic casserole or 13" by 9" glass baking dish. In microwave-safe medium bowl, heat remaining 1 tablespoon butter in microwave oven on High 15 to 20 seconds, until melted, swirling bowl once. Add bread crumbs; stir until well combined.

4. In large bowl, with mixer at high speed, beat egg whites until stiff peaks form when beaters are lifted. With rubber spatula, gently fold one third of whites into cooled cheese mixture. Fold cheese mixture gently back into remaining whites.

5. Pour mixture into prepared casserole. Sprinkle crumb mixture on top. Bake until top is browned and knife inserted in center comes out clean, about 40 minutes. Serve immediately.

**EACH SERVING:** About 190 calories, 9g protein, 9g carbohydrate, 13g total fat (7g saturated), 2g fiber, 131mg cholesterol, 280mg sodium

# Vegetable Cobbler

*Winter vegetables are roasted until tender, then bathed in a lightened cream sauce (no cream here—it's made with low-fat milk) and topped with biscuit dough that's baked to golden-brown goodness.*

**ACTIVE TIME:** 15 minutes
**TOTAL TIME:** 1 hour 30 minutes

**MAKES:** 6 main-dish servings

1 medium butternut squash (1¾ pounds), peeled, seeded, and cut into 1½-inch chunks

3 large red potatoes (1 pound), cut into 1½-inch chunks

3 medium parsnips (8 ounces), peeled and cut into 1-inch pieces

1 medium red onion, cut into 6 wedges

2 tablespoons olive oil

¾ teaspoon salt

½ teaspoon dried tarragon

1 can (14½ ounces) vegetable broth

½ teaspoon freshly grated lemon peel

1 small bunch broccoli (12 ounces), cut into 2" by 1" pieces

½ cup plus ⅔ cup low-fat milk (1%)

1 tablespoon cornstarch

1¾ cups all-purpose baking mix

½ cup cornmeal

¾ teaspoon coarsely ground black pepper

1. Preheat oven to 450°F. In shallow 3½- to 4-quart casserole or 13" by 9" glass baking dish, toss squash, potatoes, parsnips, onion, oil, salt, and tarragon until well coated with oil. Bake until vegetables are fork-tender and lightly browned, about 1 hour, stirring once.

2. After vegetables have cooked 45 minutes, in 3-quart saucepan, heat broth and lemon peel to boiling over high heat. Add broccoli; heat to boiling. Reduce heat to low; cover and simmer broccoli 1 minute.

3. In cup, with fork or wire whisk, stir ½ cup milk with cornstarch until blended. Stir milk mixture into broccoli mixture, stirring constantly, until mixture boils and thickens slightly; boil 1 minute. Pour broccoli mixture over vegetables; stir until brown bits are loosened from bottom of casserole.

4. In medium bowl, mix baking mix, cornmeal, pepper, and remaining ⅔ cup milk until just combined. Drop 12 heaping spoonfuls of biscuit dough on top of vegetable mixture. Let cobbler continue to bake until biscuits are browned, about 15 minutes.

**EACH SERVING:** About 395 calories, 11g protein, 67g carbohydrate, 11g total fat (2g saturated), 8g fiber, 5mg cholesterol, 940mg sodium

## COOK'S TIP

Leaving the skin on potatoes during cooking is the best way to conserve their nutrients. If peeling, keep the peels as thin as possible.

# Three-Bean and Wild-Rice Casserole

*Here's a wonderful main course, a creamy combination of mushrooms, wild rice, and protein-rich legumes.*

**ACTIVE TIME:** 25 minutes
**TOTAL TIME:** 1 hour 45 minutes

**MAKES:** 6 main-dish servings

1 tablespoon vegetable oil

4 medium carrots, peeled and cut into ¼-inch-thick slices

1 large onion (12 ounces), thinly sliced

1 package (10 ounces) mushrooms, trimmed and cut into ¼-inch-thick slices

¾ teaspoon salt

1 can (10¾ ounces) condensed cream of mushroom soup

3¼ cups water

1½ cups wild rice (8 ounces)

1 can (15 to 19 ounces) red kidney beans

1 can (15 to 19 ounces) Great Northern or white kidney beans (cannellini)

1 package (10 ounces) frozen baby lima beans, thawed

½ teaspoon coarsely ground black pepper

**1.** Preheat oven to 400°F.

**2.** In 12-inch skillet, heat oil over medium-high heat until hot. Add carrots, onion, mushrooms, and salt, and cook until vegetables are golden.

**3.** Meanwhile, in 2-quart saucepan over medium-high heat, heat undiluted cream of mushroom soup and water to boiling over high heat.

**4.** In deep 2½-quart casserole, stir carrot mixture, hot soup mixture, and wild rice. Cover and bake 1 hour.

**5.** Rinse and drain kidney and Great Northern beans. Stir kidney, Great Northern, and lima beans and pepper into casserole; cover and bake until hot, about 20 minutes longer. Stir before serving.

**EACH SERVING:** About 490 calories, 24g protein, 90g carbohydrate, 7g total fat (1g saturated), 20g fiber, 0g cholesterol, 1,030mg sodium

# Couscous-Stuffed Artichokes Ⓥ

*Instead of topping your grains with veggies, why not fill your veggies with whole-grain goodness?*

**ACTIVE TIME:** 1 hour | **TOTAL TIME:** 1 hour 15 minutes

**MAKES:** 4 main-dish servings or 8 side-dish servings

4 large artichokes

3 tablespoons olive oil

2 medium carrots, peeled and diced

2 garlic cloves, minced

¼ cup chopped fresh mint

3 tablespoons chopped fresh parsley

1 cup whole-wheat couscous
  (Moroccan pasta)

1½ cups vegetable broth

½ teaspoon salt

¼ teaspoon coarsely ground black pepper

1 lemon, cut into wedges

parsley sprigs for garnish

1. Prepare and cook artichokes (see Artichoke Know-How, opposite).

2. Meanwhile, preheat oven to 400°F.

3. In nonstick 10-inch skillet, heat 1 tablespoon oil over medium heat until hot. Add carrots and cook until tender, about 10 minutes, stirring occasionally. Stir in garlic; cook 1 minute longer. Remove to medium bowl. Dice artichoke stems; add to carrot mixture with mint and parsley.

4. Prepare couscous as label directs but use 1 cup broth in place of water. When couscous is done, stir in salt, pepper, carrot mixture, and remaining 2 tablespoons oil.

5. Pour remaining ½ cup broth into shallow baking dish large enough to hold all artichokes (13" by 9"); arrange cooked artichokes in dish. Spoon couscous mixture between artichoke leaves and into center cavities. Bake until artichokes are heated through, 15 to 20 minutes.

6. Serve artichokes with lemon wedges and garnish with parsley sprigs.

**EACH MAIN-DISH SERVING:** About 350 calories, 11g protein, 54g carbohydrate, 11g total fat (2g saturated), 12g fiber, 4mg cholesterol, 600mg sodium

# ARTICHOKE KNOW-HOW

When shopping, look for artichokes that are compact, firm, and heavy for their size. They're at their peak in April and May. In spring and summer, choose those with an even green color. In fall and winter, it's okay to buy artichokes with touches of light brown or bronze on the outer leaves, caused by frost (which doesn't affect the flavor). Artichokes range in size from baby (2 to 3 ounces) to jumbo (15 to 20 ounces), but size is not a sign of maturity; they're all fully grown when picked. Cooked or raw, they keep for a week in the refrigerator.

**TO PREPARE ARTICHOKES FOR COOKING:**

1. With sharp knife, cut 1 inch straight across the top. Cut off the stem so the artichoke can stand upright. Peel the stem.
2. Pull off the outer dark green leaves from the artichoke bottom. With kitchen shears, trim the thorny tips of the leaves.
3. Spread the artichoke open and carefully cut around the choke with a small knife, then scrape out the center petals and fuzzy center portion with a teaspoon and discard. Rinse the artichoke well. (You can remove the choke after cooking, but you have to wait till the artichoke cools a bit.)

**TO COOK ARTICHOKES:**

In a 5-quart saucepot, heat *1 tablespoon fresh lemon juice* and *1 inch water* to boiling over high heat. Set the *artichokes* on their stem ends in the boiling water, along with the peeled stems; heat to boiling. Reduce the heat to low; cover and simmer until a knife inserted in the center goes through the bottom easily, adding more boiling water if it evaporates, 30 to 40 minutes. Drain.

# Zucchini Halves with Couscous and Corn Ⓥ

*This calls for big Israeli couscous, but if you can't find it, use the regular kind.*

**ACTIVE TIME:** 35 minutes
**TOTAL TIME:** 1 hour 15 minutes
**MAKES:** 8 side-dish servings

- 5 teaspoons olive oil
- 4 small zucchini (6 ounces each), stems trimmed and each cut lengthwise in half
- 2 medium shallots, minced (about ¼ cup)
- ¼ teaspoon salt
- 1½ cups corn kernels (cut from 3 medium ears of corn)
- ¾ cup Israeli couscous
- ¾ teaspoon ground cumin
- 1¼ cups vegetable broth
- ½ cup water
- 2 tablespoons chopped fresh parsley
- diced tomatoes and sage sprigs for garnish

**1.** Preheat oven to 425°F. Grease broiling pan with 2 teaspoons oil. With spoon, scoop out flesh from each zucchini half, leaving about ¼-inch-thick shell. Coarsely chop zucchini flesh and set aside. Place zucchini halves, cut-side down, in broiling pan; set aside.

**2.** In nonstick 12-inch skillet, heat 2 teaspoons oil over medium heat until hot. Add shallots and cook 2 minutes, stirring. Increase heat to medium-high; add reserved chopped zucchini and salt, and cook until liquid evaporates and zucchini begins to brown, about 8 minutes. Add corn and cook 2 minutes, stirring. Transfer mixture to small bowl.

## IT'S SO GOOD!

At the height of summer, zucchini can kind of be like the guest who wouldn't go home. But it deserves much more respect than that. Summer squash supplies a variety of nutritional goodies, including bone-building calcium, manganese, magnesium, phosphorous, and vitamin A, as well as protein, iron, potassium, and vitamin C.

**3.** To same skillet, add couscous and remaining 1 teaspoon oil. Reduce heat to low; cook 2 minutes, stirring. Add cumin and cook 1 minute longer, stirring. Add broth and water; heat to boiling over medium-high heat. Reduce heat to low; cover and simmer until liquid is absorbed and couscous is tender, about 25 minutes.

**4.** Meanwhile, place zucchini halves in oven and roast until tender and edges are browned, about 15 minutes.

**5.** Return corn mixture to skillet with couscous; stir in parsley and heat through. Place zucchini halves on platter; fill with couscous and corn mixture. Sprinkle with tomato and garnish with sage sprigs.

**EACH SERVING:** About 145 calories, 5g protein, 25g carbohydrate, 3g total fat (1g saturated), 2g fiber, 0mg cholesterol, 200mg sodium